T0327471

# CAPITAL PROJECTS

# CAPITAL PROJECTS

WHAT EVERY EXECUTIVE
NEEDS TO KNOW *to*
AVOID COSTLY MISTAKES *and*
MAKE MAJOR INVESTMENTS PAY OFF

PAUL BARSHOP

WILEY

Published by John Wiley & Sons, Inc., Hoboken, New Jersey.
Published simultaneously in Canada.

For general information on our other products and services or for technical support, please contact our Customer Care Department within the United States at (800) 762-2974, outside the United States at (317) 572-3993 or fax (317) 572-4002.

Wiley publishes in a variety of print and electronic formats and by print-on-demand. Some material included with standard print versions of this book may not be included in e-books or in print-on-demand. If this book refers to media such as a CD or DVD that is not included in the version you purchased, you may download this material at http://booksupport.wiley.com. For more information about Wiley products, visit www.wiley.com.

*Library of Congress Cataloging-in-Publication Data:*

Names: Barshop, Paul H., 1964- author.
Title: Capital projects : what every executive needs to know to avoid costly mistakes, and make major investments pay off / Paul H. Barshop.
Description: Hoboken, New Jersey : John Wiley & Sons, Inc., [2016] | Includes index.
Identifiers: LCCN 2016018922 | ISBN 9781119119210 (cloth) | ISBN 9781119119241 (epub) | ISBN 9781119119234 (epdf) | ISBN 9781119176718 (obook)
Subjects: LCSH: Capital investments. | Project management.
Classification: LCC HD39 .B3185 2016 | DDC 658.15/2—dc23 LC record available at https://lccn.loc.gov/2016018922

Printed in the United States of America

10 9 8 7 6 5 4 3 2 1

# CONTENTS

## 8　It's Going to Cost How Much!?! A Guide to Help Executives Avoid Capital Cost Surprises　　**125**

## 9　Using a Project Steering Committee to Improve Executive Decision Making　　**147**

## 10　Risk Management: A Mechanism to Understand Project Risk and Decide What to Do　　**159**

## 11　Approve, Recycle, Cancel, or Hold: Making Good Stage-Gate Decisions　　**173**

# ACKNOWLEDGMENTS

I would not have been able to write this book without the support of three people. First, I dedicate this book to my wife, Cathy, the love of my life, for her encouragement, patience, and sacrifice. Second, Margaret Walker, Vice President, Engineering Solutions and Technology Centers, Dow Chemical Company (ret.), for her input and guidance. Thanks, Coach. Ed Merrow, founder, CEO, and President of Independent Project Analysis, for his leadership and the time I needed to do this project. Ed was also one of the primary reviewers for each chapter and provided, as usual, tremendous insight.

I was extremely fortunate to work closely with two highly skilled practitioners as I wrote the book. Each provided essential input to all of the chapters. The first is Ken Kallaher, Corporate Fellow at exp. Ken is an expert on the design and operation of capital project development and delivery systems. The second is Charles (Chuck) Greco, Head of Refinery and Market Projects North America, BP (ret.). Chuck is one the best project directors/managers I have ever worked with. I thank both for their commitment to the book.

I wish to thank my colleagues that I worked with throughout this project. Cheryl Burgess edited, reedited, and edited again each chapter. Qiang Qian prepared much of the quantitative analysis contained in the book. Kelli Ratliff created most of the graphics used in each chapter.

Others that made significant contributions include Richard Narramore, Senior Editor, Business Publications, Wiley; and John K. Hollman, Owner, Validation Estimating LLC. I also wish to thank

Dean Findley, Allison Aschman, Sarah Sparks, Felix Parodi, Luke Wallace, Geoff Emeigh, Charlotte Kirkpatrick, Pam Emons, Jessica Morales, and Sarah Barshop for their help with the book.

Finally, I want to thank all the executives and project professionals I have met over my 22 years at IPA performing project evaluations, research studies, and consulting engagements. There have been countless hours spent talking about all the dimensions of capital projects. I truly admire the knowledge, skills, and dedication required to make a capital project successful.

# 1 Falling Short of Expectations

How Executives Struggle to Deliver the Value
from Their Capital Projects

E xecutives often start out with high hopes for their capital projects, only to have them fall short of expectations. Capital projects are investments of substantial company resources to develop, to improve, or to refurbish an asset that is expected to generate cash flows for more than one year. Only 60 percent of finished projects actually meet all objectives after the project is complete and the asset was put into service.[1] The success rate is not much better than a coin flip. The complaints about projects range from business cases ruined by cost overruns, to market windows missed because the project was late, to assets that did not perform as expected and that are expensive to operate.

As an executive responsible for capital, you do not have to accept these results. Success or failure is not random. I will show you what you can do to increase the probability of a successful project, make your project portfolio pay off as expected, and, critically, reduce the chances of the disaster project that loses all the capital investment and gets executives fired. The road to success starts with you. Success will require your active leadership and participation in the projects that you are sponsoring or that your organization has a major role in.

How do executives cause projects to fail? Here is a real example. A company initiated a small project to boost operating margins by consolidating production at one factory. The plan was to relocate some equipment from an older factory to a newer one before shutting down and selling the old factory. The project had a very strong business case and was expected to pay back its investment in less than a year. A critical success factor for the project was to have the consolidated facility up and running in time for a three-month production period

---

[1]Results from Independent Project Analysis (IPA) project database.

when the factory would be run at full capacity. The factory was used to process an agricultural product, and the new factory had to be ready for the harvest. The project was a failure because the consolidated factory was only able to run at half capacity during the production window. The business needed three supplemental projects to finally bring the facility up to full capacity.

So, what happened? How did this project turn out to be a failure—and why were the executives in charge responsible? Many mistakes were made, but the most important one was that the executives delayed the start of the project so that the older facility could finish a production run. Another bad decision was not allowing the project team to get input from the operators of the old factory because of the sensitivities of shutting down the old factory where people were about to lose their jobs. The late start caused mistakes in the technical design because of the rush to get the work done. And because the team could not work with the factory operators, they had to make assumptions about how the equipment would be reused—and those assumptions turned out to be wrong.

The root cause of the failure was that the executives never reconciled the conflict in their objectives. On one hand, they wanted to keep the old factory running and delay the announcement of the closing for as long as possible. On the other hand, they wanted the consolidated factory up and running in time for an important seasonal window. The desire to achieve both objectives is understandable. Executives face tremendous pressure to deliver value from capital. Delivering that value often requires meeting targets that are hard to achieve. In this case, the executives should have acknowledged the risk in the objectives and developed a strategy to reduce the risk. The mitigation would have lengthened the payback period but would have still allowed for a profitable project. Instead, the business lost money on the investment.

## Background and Basis for the Book

At Independent Project Analysis, Inc. (IPA), we have been studying the problem of how businesses can maximize the value created by their capital projects for nearly 30 years. That is our mission. Our quantitative benchmarking services are used by the world's largest industrial companies as the core of their continuous improvement programs to derive more value from their projects. IPA's empirical research has led to the widespread adoption of project management concepts such as Front-End Loading (FEL) and Value Improving Practices (VIPs). The work of IPA's founder, Edward W. Merrow, has become the de facto handbook for the development and execution of megaprojects.[2]

For the past 22 years, I have worked directly with IPA clients all over the world evaluating projects and providing guidance on how to improve both individual projects and project systems. About eight years ago, I started a series of studies on the initial stages of capital project development. A capital project starts with an idea that a business need exists. Unfortunately, fully developed, viable projects do not fall from trees. There is hard work to be done to shape and define opportunities into projects that deliver sufficient benefits to justify the cost and risk. I have always been fascinated with these activities and, in particular, how a business and project organization should work together to translate a set of objectives for growth and profit into a doable project. Throughout this book, I will describe the executive's crucial role in capital project development as well as the steps necessary to ensure that the project organization listens carefully and fully to what the business needs.

---

[2]Edward W. Merrow, *Industrial Megaprojects: Concepts, Strategies, and Practices for Success* (Hoboken, NJ: Wiley, 2011).

## Capital Projects Create Value

Capital projects are high-risk, high-reward activities for both the company and the executives involved with the project. Project success is critical to the long-term financial success of a company. Projects can be a business's main engine for profitable organic growth by introducing new products or services or by increasing the production capacity of existing products and services. For example, a financial services company may have invented a new algorithm for web-based investment advice but still needs to design the application and deploy the IT infrastructure to handle the expected growth in customers. A specialty chemical company may have struck an advantageous marketing deal with a foreign partner but now needs to build a plant to make the product. A manufacturing company may have spent years developing a new technology that will cut production costs in half, allowing it to undercut its competition and take market share, but needs to build a factory to deploy the technology. Projects can also make a business more efficient or solve nagging problems. For example, a project might purchase and deploy new software systems that make the company's sales force better. Even seemingly mundane projects to upgrade or refurbish existing assets represent significant commitments of capital that need to pay off to keep the company competitive.

Capital projects actually create value when the benefits from the asset created or modified by the project exceed the project cost. The most common method for measuring the added value of a project is the net present value (NPV) generated by the investment. The formal definition of NPV is the present value of future cash flows discounted at the appropriate cost of capital, minus the initial net cash outlay. More simply, NPV is the amount of shareholder wealth created from a capital investment after accounting for the total cost of the investment and the time value of money. For example, a $10 million capital project that generates $1 million in NPV has enriched the company owners by $1 million. Positive NPV from a capital investment is a good thing. Unfortunately, it is entirely possible for a capital project to make shareholders worse off than when they started. About one in seven projects will lose all of that $10 million capital investment.

## Most Projects Create Less Value Than Expected

Executives approve or reject capital projects based on the project's expected value. The financial gap between what was expected from a capital project when it was approved and what was actually achieved can be measured. The average project delivers 22 percent less NPV than what was forecasted when the project was funded. That is what we at IPA found in a study of 431 completed industrial sector capital projects. The business goal for each project was to increase profits by adding new production or manufacturing capacity.[3] The 22 percent NPV erosion means a project targeting profit of $1 million would come out only $780,000 ahead on average.

The good news is that the average project is profitable; otherwise, everyone would be bankrupt! The bad news is that the promised profitability is often missed by a large and highly unpredictable margin.

## Results Apply to All Types of Projects

The results of this study of industrial projects are important to you even if you are not an executive involved in a multimillion-dollar project to build a new factory. The conclusion that capital projects often fall short of delivering the expected business value applies to any

---

[3]The projects were from 64 different companies in 11 different industrial sectors, located across the globe, and ranging in size from $100 million to $20 billion.

type of project. It does not matter whether the project is to construct a new office building or to develop new software. In fact, the performance of capital projects done by companies with less experience and less infrastructure for doing projects is probably a lot worse. The industrial companies in my study are capital intensive, spending hundreds of millions and in many cases billions in capital every year to build new or to refurbish their assets. Despite the importance of capital to their long-term success, these companies still struggle to consistently deliver the expected business value from their projects. Imagine the challenge for the executives of a company that only does the occasional capital project!

## Sources of Value Erosion Are Not Limited to Cost and Schedule Overruns

Value erosion occurs when what was actually delivered by a project is lower than what was promised when the project was funded. Cost and schedule overruns are usually thought of as the main culprit of value erosion, and they do indeed make a significant contribution to lower NPV, but the largest source of value erosion for these industrial projects has nothing to do with how the project was managed. The breakdown of value erosion falls into three categories in order of importance: (1) demand for the product was lower than expected, (2) the cost and/or schedule were overrun, or (3) the facility did not operate as expected. Any single project may have done well in one or two areas but fell short in others. These are just the averages for each category (see Table 1.1).

Some of the reasons people gave for the lack of demand include:

- "Lost our biggest customer."
- "Orders were lower than expected."
- "Prices were not high enough to keep the plant running."

Table 1.1  Average Value Loss by Category

| | |
|---|---|
| Expected value | 100% |
| Lower sales | −10% |
| Cost and schedule overruns | −7% |
| Asset performance shortfalls | −5% |
| Actual value delivered | 78% |

Changes in economic conditions, competitor actions, and shifting customer preferences are outside executives' control, and they make demand and price forecasts inherently uncertain, especially in the short term. Yet overconfidence in the market forecast by executives is a common source of value erosion, especially for projects that destroyed all the capital invested. The project sponsors are so certain about the revenue forecast that they are willing take on the risk of a significant cost overrun to accelerate the schedule to meet a market window when demand or prices are expected to rise rapidly. The value erosion caused by the cost and schedule overruns is doubly painful when demand is lower than expected.

What executives *do* control is the quality of the work behind the market forecast used to justify the project. In Chapter 3, I will show you that projects based on rigorous market analyses are 30 percent less likely to face a lack of demand. In other words, the chances of building unneeded capacity are much lower if executives establish requirements for developing a reliable market forecast and check that the requirements are met.

The average project erodes 5 percent of value because the production facility built by the project cannot produce what the business needs. For example, a software application may not meet all the service-level requirements established by a business. Responsibility for asset performance shortfalls is usually shared among all the groups involved in the project. Sometimes the asset could not make the product because it was never designed for that capability. The project sponsor may not have communicated the requirements clearly to the project team. It is also true that project teams sometimes do not hear what the sponsor is saying. Other times, the shortfall is due to innovative technology not working as well as expected. The technology executive may have downplayed the technical risk of the innovation. Finally, the shortfalls may occur because of mistakes made in the design or construction of the facility, often the result of a project trying to cut corners or go faster to meet the cost and schedule targets set by executives.

The results of the study show that responsibility for value erosion is shared across the organization. They also mean that fixing the problem involves executives across the organization working to improve their own areas as well as how their group interacts with others to create a common understanding as a project is developed and executed.

## How to Deliver the Value Promised

The proven processes to create more business value from investments and prevent value erosion are well known and largely accepted, at least on the surface. Three-quarters of IPA's clients have a perfectly serviceable capital project development and delivery process. I will go into more detail in the next chapter, but the process covers the entire life cycle of the project from inception to the point when the asset is put in service. Let's say R&D is finishing up the development of a new product and a new manufacturing facility is needed to make the product. The usual process for creating an asset combines a set of defined development stages with decision gates at the end of each stage. The stage-gate process for this opportunity starts when someone is assigned to investigate ways to produce the new product. The process ends when the factory is in service. The stages sequence work

**Table 1.2 Projects That Meet the Stage-Gate Process Require-
ments Tend to Deliver the Expected Value**

| | Met All Requirements | Met Some Requirements | Did Not Meet Any Requirements |
|---|---|---|---|
| Value delivery (Actual NPV/Expected NPV) | +5% | −22% | −45% |

in the order needed to identify and deliver value, and the gates allow
executives to control the project's progress through the process. The
process is managed by a project governance structure that assigns
different executives specific roles and responsibilities, creating the
checks and balances needed for good project decision making.

There isn't even much debate company-to-company on what the
process should look like. Although there are some differences to
accommodate a particular industry, there is very little substantive
difference in the fundamental approach companies take toward capital
project development.

Moreover, the process works—when it is used correctly. Projects
that followed a process, on average, actually added slightly more
value than what was forecast when the project was funded, while
projects that did not meet any of the process requirements eroded
about half the expected NPV (see Table 1.2). The average 22 percent
value erosion shows that most projects sort of muddle through,
meeting some requirements while not meeting others.

The assets created by projects that followed the process were
much less likely to face a lack of demand, have cost and schedule
overruns, or have performance issues. Critically important to
understand is that there are no average differences in the market risk
and external project risk faced by the projects in the three categories.
That is, the projects that met all the requirements were not any less
complex or inherently less risky than those that did not. Rather, using

the stage-gate process effectively allowed executives to navigate through the complexity, address risks, and deliver better results. Throughout the book, I am going to give specific examples, both good and bad, to illustrate how you can use the process to get better results for your projects.

## Causes of Value Erosion Often Start Early

One of the key findings of the research I have completed at IPA is that the quality of the starting point is a very strong predictor of the project's eventual business success. You can think about the sequence of activities in the stage-gate process in the following way: identify the business need, choose the preferred solution for meeting the business need, plan the project, do the project, and put the asset into service. Put more succinctly, the sequence is ready, aim, fire.

The beginning of a project establishes a trajectory that is difficult to change once the project gains momentum. First, projects are progressively defined, meaning details are continually added to work that was done previously. Mistakes made in the technical design, project strategies, and foundational project scope tend to cascade through the entire project life cycle. Making changes later almost always leads to costly rework and mistakes from overlooked details.

Once a project builds momentum, it is also hard to stop even if the project has a marginal value. Projects build momentum as more individuals become invested in their outcomes. The business executives sponsoring the project are usually counting on the project to improve the business's financial performance. The technology group may be keenly interested in demonstrating its research commercially. The project manager and the rest of the project professionals also have a vested interest in the project continuing and often become advocates for the project. Projects also gain financial momentum as more money is invested to complete project definition. There is a reluctance to incur the sunk costs from canceling a project just before full-funds authorization, when the full budget to complete the project is released to the project team. For example, the business may have spent a million dollars developing the project. Canceling the project means throwing away that money.

Executives throughout a company have a huge influence on how well the initial work on a project is done. My research shows that the early stages of the capital project life cycle tend to be done with less rigor and discipline than the later stages. Executives just do not pay enough attention to the formative stages of the project. The problem is a little like diet and exercise. We all know that a balanced diet and exercise are key ingredients to good health. Yet—as most of us know from personal experience—we do not always do what we know is right. To make the effort easier, I will provide practical guidance on what executives can do to improve results without overburdening them with work that adds no business value.

# 2 Why the Stage-Gate Process Is the Best Tool Executives Can Use to Get the Most Value from Their Capital Projects

I was once presenting to the CEO of a medium-sized manufacturing company and his executive team on how they could improve the results of their capital projects. Some of their recent projects had not gone so well. About five minutes into the briefing, one of his lieutenants muttered, "Oh no—not another presentation about the stage-gate process!" "Well, yes," I said, "that is a big part of what I am going to talk about." He rolled his eyes and spent most of the time checking his e-mail on his phone while I talked. Yes, the stage-gate process is old hat, but the fact is it is the only approach that has ever been shown to work long term.

A more complete name is the stage-gate project development and delivery process (see Figure 2.1). The process contains five distinct stages with gates between the first three stages, which are referred to as the *front end* of the process. Each stage has a set of requirements for the work to be completed in that stage. That work is used by executives at each stage-gate to decide whether the potential benefit from the project justifies the expense for completing the next stage. The Define gate is the point in the process when executives authorize the full budget to complete the project.

Negative reactions from executives about the stage-gate process, like the one I encountered, are not uncommon and are somewhat understandable. The objections include: "Why does it take so damn long?" Projects are complex and must be carefully planned and executed so that the asset created by the project meets specifications

**Figure 2.1  Stage-Gate Project Development and Delivery Process**

and is completed within a cost budget and time frame. The work required to achieve these goals just takes time. Executives can get frustrated by the time needed especially when they are racing to meet a market window or some other commitment. It may feel like it is taking longer because the work in the early stages is more deliberate, but using the stage-gate process effectively shaves about 25 percent off the project life cycle through better planning, reduced rework, and superior risk management.

Another objection is: "Why must I spend so much money developing the project before I even know whether I want to do it?" The process is guilty as charged on this objection. As I will discuss later, a rule of thumb is that about 5 percent of the total project budget will be spent to get to the Define gate, where executives make the final authorization decision. That money has to be written off as an expense if the project is not funded. However, there are two counters to this objection. First, good use of the process will reduce the number of projects that get all the way to the Define gate before they are stopped. Projects with weak business cases are stopped early before much money is spent. Second, on a portfolio basis, the cost of an occasional project being canceled is quickly recouped by lower spending on projects that do make it to the Execute stage because the work is done more efficiently.

Sometimes the objection is: "The project manager is always telling me I cannot make any changes once I make a decision on something." This is not true. Executives can decide to make any changes they want. What the project manager is probably trying to tell you is that the change is going to be costly and may delay the project. The rub with the stage-gate process is that the definition of the project gets progressively more detailed through the project life cycle, with each step building on the previous work. Think about it this way. Say you were building a house. The whole design was complete, and you were ready to start building the house, but then you decided to rearrange the floor plan. Much of the work that was done to detail out the original floor plan would have to be redone, wasting money and time. Sometimes change is unavoidable. We live in a dynamic world, and unexpected events in the business environment can force changes to the project. However, used properly, the stage-gate process will reduce the frequency of late change to the absolute minimum.

A final objection is: "The project manager tells me there is still a chance the project will overrun and the schedule will slip even though the process was followed!" This is also true. Cost and schedule estimates contain uncertainty. They are predictions or forecasts of what we think it will cost and how long we think it will take, not guarantees. However, the chances and magnitude of overruns are lower when the process is followed. As I showed in the previous chapter, projects that meet the requirements of the process typically deliver the promised value, while those that do not erode value.

## A Necessary Process

The stage-gate process is the best tool for achieving *all the goals* executives have for capital project investment:

- Directing capital to the most attractive, most important investment opportunities
- Maximizing the value from each capital project that is funded
- Controlling the risk of financial loss or reputational damage

Each goal is important for the long-term success of any business, large or small. The stage-gate process provides the platform for choosing the highest-priority projects and extracting as much as possible from each project that is funded, while protecting shareholders by keeping the risk profile for each project in check. Despite attempts to find a better way to develop and deliver capital projects, the result always ends up with the same stages, same gates, and same basic governance structure.

## How Does the Process Work?

The process contains five distinct stages sequenced in a specific order. The process is easy to understand as a basic concept. This is how you would use the stage-gate process to plan and take a big vacation.

**Assess** Answer some basic questions about the vacation. What do you want to do on vacation? Do you want to relax on a beach, climb a mountain, or some combination of both? When can you go on vacation? How much money do you want to spend? Using this information, you find three or four different locations that you think will provide the most enjoyment for your budget. If you are happy with the options and believe at least one of the options will work, move to the next phase.

**Select** Evaluate the different locations by getting some more information, especially the cost for each. Then, chose a location and do a little more planning so that you get a good idea of the final cost. If the cost is still okay, move to the next phase.

**Define** Finish planning the vacation by selecting flights, hotels, and transportation. You might even plan some excursions. At the end of this stage, if the cost is still acceptable, buy your tickets and make your deposits.

**Execute** Take the vacation. Spend your money but stay on budget. Enjoy yourself but make sure you make it back to the airport in time for the flight home.

**Operate** Go back to work refreshed and more productive than ever.

Really, that is it in a nutshell. I just described the sequence of activities you should follow if you want the best *chance* of having a great vacation. You start out thinking broadly about what you want from a vacation and about some of your constraints like the budget and time available. Next, you think about different alternatives that will maximize the value (or give you the best bang for your buck). Then you evaluate and decide which one is best. You plan the vacation for the option you choose, and, finally, you take the vacation.

Of course, there is no guarantee it will turn out to be the best vacation. It could rain or you could get sick. Also, you could skip all the planning and wake one morning and buy a ticket somewhere that looks fun and have the best vacation of your life. The chances of that happening are lower, but there is always a chance.

I also have left out some of the things that could make planning this vacation more complicated. The process is not as linear as I suggest. There may be some back-and-forth in the early stages. For example, you might identify some locations you want to go to but all are too expensive. You either have to increase the budget or change your expectations for the vacation. If you were planning a vacation for your family, you would have to consider what they like to do when considering different options. Now the calculus for maximizing value gets a lot more difficult. You have to balance multiple objectives and figure out the vacation that will best satisfy all the objectives, knowing that not everyone will be fully happy. You also have to consider the risk of different locations in your assessment. Say there is a location that you really prefer, but the cost is outside your price range unless you go during the rainy season. You have to weigh whether the risk of rain spoiling your fun is worth the potential reward if it does not rain.

Capital projects are more complex than planning a vacation, which is why following the stage-gate process is even more important. The sequence of activities in the process is designed to handle the complexity of project decision making by organizing it into a logical sequence and breaking it into manageable pieces.

You might notice that the description of the Assess stage in my example has the most content and that each subsequent stage description has less and less information. By the time I get to the Operate stage, I summarize its purpose in one line! The content of this book mirrors that pattern. In fact, I have not included any discussion of the Execute or the Operate stages in the book. The reason for this is simple. The executive role is focused heavily on the first three stages of the project life cycle, especially the Assess stage. By the time a project gets to the Execute stage, there should be little executive involvement other than monitoring performance and being ready to step in if there are problems.

### Assess: What Do We Want to Accomplish?

Assess is the most important stage for executives because it sets the path for the entire project. Let's take a simple example in which the sales forecast for one of a business's core products indicates sales will grow by 25 percent over the next two years, but the business's factory is running nearly at full capacity. Executives think they can increase profits by selling more product and want to identify an approach that will generate the most profits from the expected increase in sales. The Assess stage contains a series of activities to answer the question: *What is the best way to take advantage of an opportunity or to solve a problem that will maximize value?*

The Assess stage is a deliberate approach to answering this question. The steps to do this are (1) define the opportunity, (2) define business objectives and requirements, and (3) identify alternatives for meeting the business objectives. Generally, the Assess stage ends before the preferred alternative is chosen. Executives will have to spend money to perform the technical and economic analysis to select the preferred alternative. Stopping here allows executives to decide whether the project is even feasible and worth spending the money for the next phase.

Many projects go awry in the Assess stage because this work is done poorly. Sometimes executives take what I call the just-do-it approach to a project in which the decision on how to pursue the opportunity is made very quickly. In this example, executives may decide to expand capacity by upgrading some equipment before considering some questions such as: *Should we build in some spare capacity if demand is higher than the forecast? Or, have there been any technology advances that we can adopt to improve our cost position?* Soliciting input from the technology group may open up a range of options. The problem with the just-do-it approach is that executives may miss opportunities to create more value from the project.

I have written two chapters about how to avoid problems in the Assess stage and establish a strong foundation for any project:

Chapter 3, "The Project Frame: Understand the Opportunity before Starting a Project"

Chapter 5, "The Single Most Important Thing an Executive Can Do to Make Any Capital Project Succeed: Define Clear Objectives"

## Select and Define: How Should We Accomplish It?

Once the business objectives and requirements are established in the Assess stage, a project to deliver those objectives has to be defined. Project definition is the process of converting the business objectives into a project scope and strategy to design, build, and install the asset created or modified by the project to achieve those objectives. A basic principle of project definition is that the scope and strategy gets increasingly more detailed through the Select and Define stages. I find the easiest way to explain this is to relate it to projects that you might do in your personal life. Say you are having a custom house built for you. You would probably hire an architect to design the house. During the Assess stage, you would work with the architect to select the location, the size, and the general layout of your house. This would give a rough number of how much the house is going to cost. Now the work designing the house and the planning for how the house will get built really starts. For the design, the architect probably starts with designing the foundation and placing and sizing each room. For example, you decide where the kitchen will be and how big it will be. Once you do this for all the rooms, you start adding details like paint colors, materials, location of the electrical outlets and so forth. In parallel, there is work to develop plans for who is going to build the house, how the contractor will be managed, how the materials will be ordered, and when the construction will be done.

Unlike planning and building a house, most capital projects will require a sizable project team to complete project definition and lead the Execute stage. The first step in forming the project team is the assignment of the project manager and other core personnel at or near the start of the Select stage. The composition and the size of the team will change as a project moves through the project life cycle, but the core team is expected to remain intact throughout the entire project. The project frame, objectives, and plans developed in the Assess stage are instructions to the project team on their mission. The instructions identify goals, milestones, and boundary conditions.

The most challenging aspect of project definition to executives is that changes to decisions made early in the front end may cause considerable rework and an increase in project risk. For example, say you have made it all the way through the design process and you decide to change the layout of the kitchen. Think about all the work that now has to be redone. The change may force a new layout of other rooms, which in turn may change the design of the foundation, roof, and load-bearing walls. The change may force modifications to the plans for bringing power and heat and air conditioning to each room. The changes continue to ripple through until every detail is accounted for. The consequence is that your house is delayed and you have to pay for all that rework. Change like this has a similar effect on any type of project, whether you are developing a software application or building a factory. Strong work in the Assess stage minimizes late changes because the decisions made early in the project are better. The work in the Select and Define stages is covered in these chapters:

Chapter 6, "The Executive's Role in Building and Supporting High-Performing Project Teams"

Chapter 7, "Project Definition: The Fundamental Capital Project Concept Every Executive Must Understand"

Chapter 8, "It's Going to Cost How Much!?! A Guide to Help Executives Avoid Capital Cost Surprises"

Chapter 10, "Risk Management: A Mechanism to Understand Project Risk and Decide What to Do"

## What Is the Role of Executives in the Process?

The content of this book focuses exclusively on the first three stages of the process, with a heavy emphasis on the Assess stage. This mirrors the role executives have in the process. The work of executives is most intensive early on as they set the direction of the project. Once the project moves through the Select stage, the executive role shifts to an oversight and support role. I have not explained every element of the work that takes place in the front end of the process. Instead, I have focused on what I believe executives need to know to perform their role.

Guide, supervise, and support is an apt description of the executive role. First, executives guide the development of the business case. The business case explains the business justification for the project, documents the business objectives and key performance targets, and describes, at a high level, the project's scope of work. The business case also contains the investment analysis that evaluates the project for profitability and risk.

Executives supervise the project team so that the business case is a realistic assessment of the expected value and so that the expected value is actually delivered. Some of the supervision is done directly through interaction with the project team. For example, the executive sponsoring a project will meet regularly with the project manager, getting updates on the status of the project and making decisions as necessary. Some monitoring of the project is done by others in the form of audits or project reviews, and the results are reported back to executives. For example, someone might review the completeness of the technical design and check that it is satisfactory for the particular stage in the process. The results of the review may not even be reported back if there are no problems.

Executives support the project by securing the resources the project team needs to be successful. They also use their influence to clear away barriers outside the project team's control that threaten the project. They communicate upward to more senior management to get their input and support for the project. Executive support also includes interaction with the project team to explain the importance of the project and to encourage the project team members to work through problems they are facing. The importance of their role in supporting the project is often underappreciated by executives, but it is not underappreciated by the project team!

## Different Kinds of Executives

Major investments are likely to have multiple executives involved in the project, each with different but important roles. I put executives involved in capital into three groups: executives sponsoring the project, executives supporting the project, and executives making the stage-gate decision.

- Executives *sponsoring* the project: The leader(s) of the organization advocating for the project have the responsibility for the value created by the investment. The project is being done to advance the strategies of the organization or to improve its operation. For example, a business unit is the primary proponent for an expansion of production facility. The accounting department is the driver behind replacing obsolete software. The technology group backs a new testing laboratory. A project sponsor, usually an executive role if the project is large enough, is chosen from within the organization to champion the project and to be the single point of accountability for the overall success of the project.

- Executives *supporting* the project: Other executives are stakeholders in a project. That is, they will either be affected by the project—their organization may operate the asset that is created—or they will provide services such as technology or product development or project management used to develop and execute the project. The responsibilities of the executives who support the project are twofold: (1) to support the project sponsor and help them direct the project and (2) to represent the interests of their organizations as the project is developed. Take, for example, a project installing manufacturing technology that is maintained and updated by a technology organization. The head of technology may assign and supervise resources and advise the project sponsor of any technology issues that affect the project. The technology executive also has a responsibility to protect the integrity of the technology against changes that may reduce its performance or cause a deviation from the business's long-term technology strategy.

- Executives *making the stage-gate decision*: Executives more senior than the project sponsor or even the executive who runs the organization may have the final say in whether a project is approved to move to the next stage in the stage-gate process. For example, for a major investment, representatives from office of the CEO may make the stage-gate decision. Their role is to objectively review the merits of the project and also consider the project as part of a broader portfolio.

## Project Governance Structures

The collective activity of all these executives is orchestrated in something called project governance. Project governance encompasses the rules for project decision making and defines the roles and responsibilities of all the executives involved in a project. This figure is a basic representation of the project governance structure for a capital project. The center of project governance is the project sponsor. The project sponsor is the chief proponent of the project from the organization requesting the capital for the project. The investment committee makes the stage-gate decision. As I said, their role is to objectively review the merits of the project and consider the project as part of a broader portfolio. The project steering committee is chaired by the project sponsor and staffed with the executives from the organizations that are major stakeholders in the project, typically limited to three or four (see Figure 2.2).

The governance structure can be arranged in different ways and can be scaled up or down, depending on the size and nature of the project. However it is arranged, the governance structure has to provide a set of checks and balances that allows only business cases that

**Figure 2.2  Typical Project Governance Structure**

are robust and that prudently balance cost and benefit, risk and reward through the front end of the process.

## Stage-Gates and Executive Control

The stage-gates are the mechanism for directing capital to the highest-priority projects. With the stage-gate process, work on an opportunity or problem is not even allowed to start unless executives agree that the business objective is something they want to pursue. Executives further control capital spending with the stage-gates by only releasing the money needed to complete the next stage of the process. For example, a project that has been approved to move from the Assess to Select stage only gets the budget for the Select stage, not the budget to complete the entire project. The purpose of funding only to the next gate is to ensure that the gates are meaningful decision points for executives.

The key document for any project is the business case. The business case explains the business justification for the project, documents the business objectives and key performance targets, and describes the project's scope of work. The business case also contains the investment analysis that evaluates the project for profitability and risk. Stage-gates are checkpoints built into the project delivery process that give executives the opportunity to review the business case to decide if the potential benefit from the project warrants spending more money to complete the next stage. The business case for a project becomes progressively more detailed at each stage-gate. This is how executives should think about the business case prepared at the end of each stage:

Assess Gate: Is this potentially a good investment?

Select Gate: Is this a good investment?

Define Gate: Is this still a good investment?

The initial business case prepared at the Assess gate is often based on very preliminary information and should be used to judge the feasibility of the project only. There is not enough certainty in the inputs to the investment analysis to commit to the project yet. The work in the Select stage reduces this uncertainty so that executives can decide on the project's viability. However, full funding of the project is not released until the end of the Define stage. There are two reasons for this. First, it ensures that the Define stage work is complete before the project enters the execution stage. Second, the uncertainty in the estimates used to complete the investment analysis is reduced even further. This gives executives more confidence that the business case can actually be delivered.

Weak gates are an endemic problem for the stage-gate process. The process will never work as well as it should if projects that have incomplete or marginal business cases are allowed to pass through the stage-gates. Project governance and the operation of strong stage-gates are explained in the following chapters:

Chapter 4, "The Critical Project Sponsor Role"

Chapter 9, "Using a Project Steering Committee to Improve Executive Decision Making"

Chapter 11, "Approve, Recycle, Cancel, or Hold: Making Good Stage-Gate Decisions"

# 3 The Project Frame

## Understand the Opportunity before Starting a Project

A project starts with a *frame*. A project frame is a clear explanation of the opportunity or problem being solved, what the business hopes to accomplish with the opportunity, and the plan for moving forward. As more detail is added, the project frame evolves into the initial business case prepared at the end of the Assess stage.

The value of the project frame is that it forces you to stop and think before deciding the best way to take advantage of an opportunity. It guards against our first impulse to quickly jump to a solution and move forward once an opportunity has been identified. This push to move forward quickly is understandable. We get excited about projects. Opportunities have the promise of growth and profit. Solving problems will improve margins and make running the business easier.

A strong frame also helps you avoid an exercise in wishful thinking by examining several critical questions such as: *How will we create value from this project? What competitive advantage do we have that enables us to offer a better product or service than our competition or offer the same product or service at a lower cost?* If we cannot make a case that there is a basis for creating value, the opportunity should not be pursued.

A strong frame increases the chance of someone having that "aha!" moment when a new solution that will create a much higher-level value emerges. It also guards against that "oh crap!" moment when a risk or problem that threatens success suddenly appears after a project is well down the road.

Executives do not develop the project frame; the work is delegated to someone in the business, usually a specialized resource. Even though the executive does not do all the work, the level of executive involvement is the highest and most critical during the project framing activities. The frame is your opportunity to set the foundation for work that will produce exactly what you need to get the most value from any opportunity.

Without real engagement from executives, the framing exercise adds little value—or worse—allows a project to move forward with a frame that has gaps that will result in lower value or even big losses. In my experience, the project frame is not really complete until the executives directly responsible for the project have been in the same room reviewing and challenging the contents of the frame, often over a series of meetings. The content has to be pushed around and understood before there is real agreement between executives.

## Typical Contents of a Project Frame

I am going to describe the project frame and how it is developed to show you the power of the result. Let's start with the project frame for a family-owned restaurant. The restaurant is very busy and people love the food. The owner is thinking of expanding, but growth in the area has attracted the attention of several well-established restaurant groups that are planning to open restaurants in the area. These restaurants have started in the area, are highly reviewed, and have successfully expanded over the past decade. Table 3.1 shows what a project frame for the restaurant might look like.

Without a project frame, the restaurant owner might just decide to build a new restaurant without fully considering the risk that the competition might actually take away customers. The owner may find out that the family is not really committed to running an expanded business. Without a project frame, the owner runs a much higher risk of wasting a lot of time and money working up the plans before canceling the whole venture or—even worse—financial disaster.

With a project frame, the restaurant owner has a solid platform for thinking up different options and deciding which one is the best.

**Table 3.1 Project Frame for a Family-Owned Restaurant**

| | |
|---|---|
| **External Market/ Customer Issue** | • Local population is growing rapidly; there are long waits to get a table on most nights. However, strong competition is coming that will compete for customers. |
| **Company-Specific Opportunity** | • Increase revenue and profits by adding capacity to serve more people. |
| **Boundary Conditions and Givens** | • All options should be considered: new location, expand existing restaurant, rearrange current configuration, or offer takeout service.<br>• Will not compromise the quality of food and service. |
| **Stakeholder Analysis** | • Owner's family—how much more time are they willing to commit to the business?<br>• Customers—how will they react to the changes? |
| **Risks and Uncertainties** | • Competition will really ramp up over the next 12 months and business might actually decline.<br>• Amount of money a bank will lend. |
| **Decision Criteria and Value Drivers** | • Financial payback period.<br>• Do not take on too much debt to expand.<br>• Flexibility to cut losses if new restaurants start to take too much business. |

The owner may also decide that the expansion is too risky and cancel the plans right away.

## Unlock Value by Finding a Better Option

I really like how the graph in Figure 3.1 shows one objective for doing a project frame. The goal is to find Option A, the one option that is superior to the others.

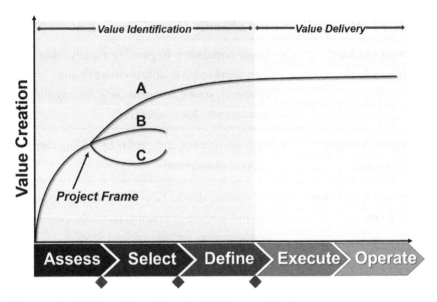

**Figure 3.1  Value Creation for Different Options**

I admit Figure 3.1 is a simplified description of the identification and selection of options. Usually the best option is not as obvious as I have shown here. The value shown on the vertical axis is more than just the expected profit from each option. There are multiple factors that determine the relative value of options besides profit. Residual risk, strategic value, and investment efficiency are also input factors executives use when choosing between options. It requires analysis of all of these factors to identify the best option.[1]

Your chances of finding Option A are much higher if you think about the opportunity fully before deciding what to do. Let's say a business forecasts that the market for its product has a healthy

---

[1] Also, I am only showing three options here. There can be more depending on the project, and for complex projects, the identification and selection of options may go through several iterations. The first set may be a high-level selection of the best location, for example. Once the location is selected, there may be multiple options for the best configuration of the asset at that location that have to be evaluated.

15 percent per year growth rate. The easiest solution is to expand the existing facility. The total cost to add capacity will be the lowest of any option and the time needed to get the capacity up and running will be the shortest. Although that solution may be the most attractive on the surface, it might be shortsighted. Perhaps a vendor has developed a new technology that cuts manufacturing costs significantly. Instead of expanding, the best long-term solution to keep the business competitive might be to build a new facility using the new technology. Perhaps there are companies that will make the product for you, avoiding a capital project all together. By establishing three distinct alternatives, the business can thoroughly evaluate each to find the superior option.

The value of the project frame is not limited to project scope. The best example of how a project frame created value that I have been personally involved with was a project that saved over $80 million, over 25 percent of the total project cost, from a strategy that emerged from a deliberate approach to frame the project. The business had to modify four existing sites to comply with new environmental requirements. Rather than approach each site as a separate project, the business developed a program that allowed it to use the same design four times, but only pay for it once. The business was not able to tailor the design for each site, which meant forgoing some operating flexibility, but the capital savings more than justified the strategy.

You might be thinking, "Well, that does not seem so difficult. It should have been obvious that a program approach could deliver huge savings." Perhaps it is obvious in hindsight, but I can tell you that not a single competitor who had to comply with the same regulations came up with a similar strategy.

## How to Develop a Project Frame

There are many different versions you can use for a project frame. The exact form depends on the nature and complexity of the project, but

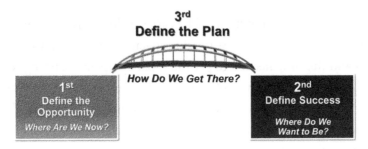

**Figure 3.2  Questions Asked and Answered in the Project Frame**

any version must address these three questions that are answered in the order listed next (see Figure 3.2):

1. Where are we now?

2. Where do we want to be?

3. How do we get there?

The order of the questions is intentional. *Where are we now?* establishes the breadth of the opportunity and the current position of the business to take advantage of the opportunity. *Where do we want to be?* defines where the business would like to be after the project is complete. You need to understand where you are *before* you can decide where you want to go otherwise you might chose a destination that is too difficult or too easy. Once you know the starting and ending points, you can start planning how to get there. I am going to give an overview of each question using examples to give you an idea of the work that needs to be done to answer each question.

## Where Are We Now?

An opportunity is created by an external or internal change. In my first example, the restaurant owner observed that business was so good that customers were having to wait a long time for a table. Opportunities are also created from internal changes. A business that develops a new or better product or manufacturing process creates an opportunity for revenue growth. Sometimes opportunities are problems that need to be fixed, such as a company's financial reporting software becoming obsolete or a factory that is not able to produce at full capacity. However the opportunity or problem is identified, the first step is to perform a market or technical analysis to really understand the opportunity.

**Make Sure There Really Is an Opportunity First** A common weakness in a project frame is that the analysis that defines the opportunity is not done rigorously enough. When this happens, the potential value from the opportunity may be overstated or the wrong solution may be pursued. Often the opportunity is stated concisely in an opportunity statement like this:

> We have the opportunity to increase revenue, profits, and our leadership position with our polymer product. The market is growing by 8 percent year, and we have a $0.25 per pound cash cost advantage compared to the next best competitor. There is also an opportunity to push into the compounded product market, a market with higher margins.

The robustness of the opportunity statement hinges on two pieces of information: (1) the market is actually growing at 8 percent and (2) the company truly has a $0.25 per pound cash cost advantage. Unfortunately, in approximately 3 out of 10 growth projects in IPA's databases, the market analysis that underpins an opportunity statement such as the one I just showed is done poorly. These projects added production capacity in anticipation of higher project demand. Projects based on weak market analyses were more than twice as likely to overestimate the demand as those that had strong analyses. Consequently, the business did not need all the extra capacity it added with the project, and the project did not generate all the value expected when the project was authorized. Let me explain further before discussing what you should do about this.

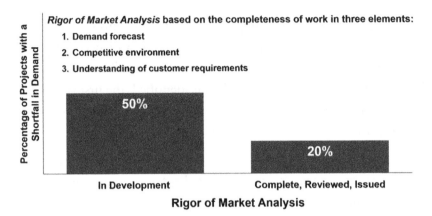

**Figure 3.3 Rigorous Market Analysis Produces More Accurate Demand Forecasts**

Figure 3.3 shows two groups: (1) projects that were still developing the market analysis at the end of the Assess stage (first bar) and (2) projects that had completed the underlying market analysis (second bar). Half of all projects in the *In Development* column suffered from a significant lack of demand during the first three years of operation after the asset was put into service. Only 20 percent of the projects that were *Complete* had a significant shortfall in demand.

**Executives Are Responsible for Confirming the Market Analysis**   This is a huge difference in results that you cannot ignore. The analysis that establishes the opportunity has to be done thoroughly before a project frame is complete.

There is an equivalent to a market analysis for any type of project. The justification for a public sector project to build a new road has to be underpinned by traffic studies verifying the need for the road. The justification for a project for new customer relationship management software has to show why and how the existing system is not meeting current needs and what other benefits are expected from the project.

Any project to fix a problem such as poor reliability has to be defended with a thorough technical analysis. Executives have to establish the requirements for the analysis underpinning the opportunity and check that the work is actually done.

**Define the Current Condition**   The opportunity definition establishes what is happening externally to the company. The *current condition* defines the business's position within that opportunity. Here is an example of an external change and a business's current condition. In 2009, the U.S. government accelerated the timetable for vehicles sold in North America to meet a 35-mile-per-gallon standard for corporate average fuel economy for new vehicles from model year 2020 to 2016. One way for automakers to meet this more stringent requirement is to use lighter-weight, higher-strength steel in their cars to reduce vehicle weight, thereby improving fuel economy. A steel company did a thorough market analysis and produced this opportunity statement:

> **Opportunity:** The current consumption of specialty steel is 500,000 tons per year. Our market analysis indicates demand will increase to 2,000,000 tons per year in the 2015 to 2020 time frame. The operating margins on specialty steel grades like this are higher than the margins of more standard grades.
>
> **Company-Specific Opportunity:** Our business does not serve this market niche.

These high-level statements were supported by an in-depth market analysis. In addition to the market forecast for demand, the company has to understand the competitive environment. Their competition undoubtedly sees the same opportunity. The company has to understand the competition's cost position and their ability to build additional capacity to supply the market. In this case, the company believed it had an advantage in the cost of production. They produce the basic steel that is made into the specialty steel at a very competitive price through the economies of scale at their existing facilities. The cost advantage, they believed, would allow them to operate profitability even if competition also built capacity to supply the market.

**Do Not Move to Solutions Yet**   The project frame here is at a critical juncture once the opportunity has been defined. At this point, executives might skip to the solution and issue some specific objectives for an independent production line:

- Build capacity to produce 250,000 tons per year of specialty steel by June 2014.

- Production costs must be at or below $10,000 per ton to ensure all capacity can be sold.

- Achieve an 18 percent internal rate of return.

- Complete product qualification with customers by the end of December 2014.

On the surface, the objectives look pretty good. They are specific and provide the project team with some clear instructions on what success looks like. The team can do economic studies for different combinations of technology and location that will meet or exceed the objectives. However, the executives skipped some important steps in developing the project if they move right from the opportunity statement to solution. They may have found "Option B," an acceptable strategy that will add value, but with some more thought and analysis, they may find "Option A."

## Where Do We Want to Be?

*Where do we want to be?* is often referred to as the *target condition* that is reached after the project is complete. The target condition is eventually defined by a set of comprehensive, quantitative objectives like I just showed, but before we get to that level of detail, the target condition must be explored through more analysis. The analysis includes the following steps:

- Define the boundary conditions and givens.
- Perform stakeholder and risk and uncertainty analysis.
- Identify decision criteria and value drivers.

**_Define the Boundary Conditions and Givens_** Executives establish the _boundary conditions_ and _givens_ for the opportunity. Boundary conditions specify the limits to the opportunity and the potential dimensions of a solution. The boundary conditions can be financial, locational, timing, technology, or whatever. Givens are absolutes that any solution cannot violate. Together they form a mandate to limit the scope of the project frame and describe the constraints under which the business case must work.

In this example, a boundary condition the steel company executives gave is a target for the cost of production at $10,000 per ton, a level low enough to allow the unit to operate profitably even at lower market prices. Another boundary condition was the maximum budget the business can afford. There is no sense in thinking up an option that includes a brand new site if the business cannot afford to pay for it. In my experience, executives are often reluctant to share the maximum budget for fear that the options presented will spend up to the limit. This fear should be unfounded if executives remain in control of the project frame and insist that a spectrum of options be prepared, not just the most expensive.

Types of givens for a project that always show up are things such as "no one gets hurt" or "we will be transparent in our dealings with the local community." These statements assert that the project will be done in a way that does not violate the company's operating principles. Other givens are specific to the opportunity. For example, a specific given for this project might be that production is available by a schedule milestone for starting up the asset or even that the project has to be authorized by a certain date.

***Stakeholder and Risk and Uncertainty Analysis***   A stakeholder is any person or organization who is affected by the opportunity and who can affect the shape of the opportunity itself. A stakeholder analysis is performed to identify all stakeholders and to rank their level of interest in the opportunity and their ability to influence the opportunity. The stakeholder analysis is a critical activity to ensure that the interests and demands of important stakeholders are included in the project frame. In this example, a key stakeholder might be the U.S. government. In particular, the government's attitude toward the steel company's entrance into the market could have a large influence on success. One concern the government might raise is that the steel company would build so much capacity that it would dominate the market and limit competition. In response to the stakeholder analysis, the executives might establish another boundary condition that limits the business's potential market share to no more than 35 percent of the total market.

The risk and uncertainty analysis identifies areas that should be factored into the target conditions, options the business might pursue, and what work must be done to evaluate options. One threat to this opportunity might be that a new U.S. president would relax the fuel economy standards or push them back to their original timetable. If this happens, the business will have capacity sitting idle because demand will increase at a slower rate than expected. The risk and uncertainty analysis might lead to executives creating a given that any solution has to be flexible enough to produce other products if demand is less than expected.

***Identify Decision Criteria and Value Drivers***   Decision criteria specify how the business will chose between options. Common decision criteria include quantitative measures such as return on investment and the level of risk. These types of criteria are not hard to understand or figure out. Executives also need to include decision criteria that are harder to measure yet still important when choosing among options. Say in this example the steel company has five locations where it could add capacity. To varying degrees, the local communities will be resistant to the expansion because it will increase air emissions, noise, and traffic around the plant. Resistance might delay the project or force the company to spend more money to expand roads or build noise barriers. The executives might include in the decision criteria a ranking of the potential resistance to the expansion when selecting a location.

Value drivers act as levers on the value created by the opportunity. For example, if the technology selected was flexible enough to produce several different grades of specialty steel, the risk of a shortfall in demand would be reduced even further. Thinking about value drivers is great for creating the conditions for an "aha!" moment. For example, I was involved with a project that listed reducing the delivery time for key pieces of equipment as a key value driver. Faster delivery would allow the business to get to the market faster. This prompted someone on the team to think about how equipment that was already on-site could be reconfigured to the new service, saving not only time but also money.

## Use the Frame for Executive Alignment and Endorsement

So much of the success of a capital project lies in communication across organizational boundaries. The project frame facilitates the conversation between the business and the other groups that will support the project. For this example, there are four groups: (1) business, (2) technology, (3) site manufacturing, and (4) project management plus senior executive management involved in developing the project frame. The business has the lead role in developing a project frame that identifies how they can make money. The technology organization has to assess different technologies. Site manufacturing has to provide information about how new production would fit into the site. Project management has to provide strategies for delivering the asset. All of these groups must have a common understanding of the opportunity so that they can collaborate effectively. The project frame is the best way to facilitate this dialog between each organization.

A basic project frame for this opportunity is shown in Table 3.2. The actual project frame for this opportunity was more detailed than

**Table 3.2  Project Frame: Supply Specialty Steel**

| | |
|---|---|
| **External Market/ Customer Issue** | • Projected demand for specialty steel is expected to increase by 2,000,000 tons per year by the 2016–2020 time frame. |
| **Company-Specific Opportunity** | • Our business does not serve this profitable market niche. |
| **Boundary Conditions and Givens** | • Product costs no more than $10,000 per ton. <br> • Capital investment cannot exceed $250 million. <br> • Investment must exceed 18 percent internal rate of return (IRR). <br> • Market share cannot exceed 25 percent of total industry demand. <br> • Acquire or build capacity by end of 2014. |
| **Stakeholder Analysis** | • U.S. government concerns about monopoly position <br> • Customer qualification of product. |
| **Risks and Uncertainties** | • Delay in fuel economy standards by new administration will delay demand for high-strength steel. <br> • Local community acceptance. |
| **Decision Criteria and Value Drivers** | • Internal rate of return. <br> • Flexibility to produce different product grades. |

what I show here. The work to build the frame required a detailed market analysis; discussion with stakeholders, including the government, customers, and local communities; technology studies; and site surveys. The project frame and the initial business case took six months to complete.

The time required for the project frame will depend on how much analysis is needed to complete the work. Answering questions such as *What is the size of the market?*, *What are competitors doing?*, and *How are customer needs changing?* may take some time. Identifying stakeholders is not that difficult. Figuring out what they want and how they can influence the opportunity may take much longer. Location information for opportunities that will build a physical asset can take many months to acquire. You have to understand things such as infrastructure availability, weather conditions, and permitting requirements before identifying and evaluating feasible options. Last, defining the current condition requires an in-depth study of what your company is actually capable of doing. Do you have the ability to deploy a more complex technology or define and execute the potential project?

The pressure to push forward before the project frame is complete is ever present. We get excited about the opportunity or we fear that if we do not move forward the opportunity will be missed. Executives must have the patience and enforce the discipline to prevent this from happening. For companies that routinely do capital projects, executives can make the activity easier and more efficient by building the capability to do the work. As one executive put it to me, the goal is to build the corporate muscle memory so that a strong frame is developed every time.

## Develop the Target Condition

A completed project frame is used to produce the target condition, the specific business goals to be achieved by pursuing the opportunity

**Table 3.3 Current and Target Condition for Project to Supply Specialty Steel**

| Current Condition | Target Condition |
|---|---|
| Current consumption of specialty strength steel is 500,000 tons per year. | • Projected demand for specialty steel is expected to quadruple by the 2016–2020 time frame. |
| Our business does not serve this market niche. | • Our business will produce enough specialty steel to serve 25 percent of the market. |
| We do not have the capacity to make this product. | • Acquire or build capacity by end of 2014. Investment must exceed 18 percent IRR. |
|  | • Production costs at or below $10,000 per ton. |
|  | • Capital project investment cannot exceed $250 million. |

(see Table 3.3). The difference between the current condition and the target condition is often referred to as the *performance gap*.

## How Do We Get There?

During the Assess stage, a number of different options were proposed for bridging the performance gap. One option the business considered but ultimately dropped was acquiring the capacity for producing the grades of specialty steel by buying a smaller company. Eventually, the options were winnowed down to three distinct alternatives:

1. Install a single production line at existing location A.

2. Install a single production line at existing location B.

3. Install two smaller production lines at location A and location B.

After the options have been identified, the initial business case is completed using one of the options as the base case. At least one of the options proposed has to meet all the boundary conditions and givens before the initial business case is presented for review and approval at the Assess stage-gate. For example, the base case for this project was the first option. It met the minimum return on investment target of 18 percent IRR and its total cost was below $250 million.

The work to evaluate the proposed options is completed in the appropriately named Select stage, the next stage of the stage-gate process when the technical and economic analysis needed to choose the best option is performed. The plan for completing the Select stage, including the evaluation and selection of the superior option, is part of the proposal made to the investment committee reviewing the initial business case. The plan identifies the data requirements for performing options analysis, the people needed, the budget, and the time required for the full stage.

The start of the Select phase is a major milestone in the project life cycle. The project team is formed and project definition begins. The project frame and the objectives that are developed as part of the initial business case are the charter for the project team. It describes the business need and guides the development of the project to meet the business need. After we discuss the role of the project sponsor in the next chapter, I will describe the process for developing clear objectives.

# 4 The Critical Project Sponsor Role

inding the project sponsor can sometimes be like that game Where's Waldo? Instead of trying to find Waldo, though, you are trying to find the one person who is accountable for the value delivered by a project. At some companies, Waldo is not even in the picture because the project sponsor role does not exist. At other companies, Waldo may appear blurry and out of focus because the role is not well defined or there is no accountability for the performance of the role. Weak project sponsorship leads to projects that do not produce as much value as they could have and projects that regularly fall short of delivering the value promised at authorization.

To understand the project sponsor role, I first need to explain what *being accountable for the value delivered by a project* actually means. I also want to emphasize that the role I am going to describe is a leadership role. Much of the project sponsorship work I describe is done by others. The project sponsor leads by guiding the work and overseeing decision making.

The accountability for delivering value breaks down into three areas (see Figure 4.1). The project sponsor is the one person who is accountable for all three areas. Having this single point of accountability is necessary to eliminate any ambiguity about who is responsible for making each happen.

**Figure 4.1 Project Sponsor Accountability**

Let's keep it simple to start. Let's say a business sees that a competitor is abandoning one of its product lines in 18 months. A quick calculation shows that the business could add $250,000 in annual profit if it could take over those sales. The problem is that the company's current capacity is nearly maxed out, so the business needs to figure how to supply the additional product. A rough estimate of the capital cost indicates that about a $1 million investment is needed to supply the additional product. The business uses a simple payback period to measure return on investment. A $1 million project that is expected to increase profits by $250,000 per year will have a payback period of four years ($1 million capital/$0.25 million profit per year = 4 years).

Right here is the first instance of accountability for delivering value. Broadly, the project sponsor is accountable for ensuring that the opportunity is real and that a project to pursue the opportunity is feasible. Is the $250,000 in annual profit realistic? Is the competitor really abandoning the product? Will the competitor's customers buy your product? Will other competitors step in? Is the $1 million cost estimate for the expansion a good estimate? Can the project be done in time to get the sales? The project sponsor is accountable for ensuring that the initial business case is not a house of cards, meaning the opportunity is real, feasible, and worth pursuing.

The next step is to figure out how to maximize the value from the opportunity. Some questions here could include: *Are there ways to reduce the capital required without jeopardizing asset performance? With the expansion, should we also make upgrades to the technology to reduce the cost of production and boost margins?* This is the next instance of accountability for delivering value. The project sponsor pushes the project team to find ways to maximize the value produced by the opportunity. In Chapter 3, I talked about the pursuit of Option A, the option that delivered superior value. It is the project sponsor who leads the effort to find Option A. The project sponsor is accountable for producing a business case that maximizes value and that balances risk and reward.

Identifying a feasible opportunity and developing a robust business case does not mean much if the value cannot actually be realized. The project manager takes the lead role in building the asset that produces the value. The accountability of the project sponsor should not be confused with the accountability of the project manager. The project manager is accountable for delivering an asset that meets specifications in a set time frame and within a certain budget. But the project sponsor is accountable for supporting and guiding the project manager so that the capital project is successful.[1] The project sponsor makes sure that all the work needed to realize the value that is outside the project manager's responsibility gets done. In this example, the project sponsor oversees and integrates any work, such as the preparation by sales to get the competitor's customers, the work by purchasing to supply more raw materials, and the logistics planning to get the products to the customer. All of this needs to come together to generate the anticipated profits.

Last, here is one example of the difference having a project sponsor made on a project IPA evaluated to prevent value from being lost.[2] The project to open a new manufacturing complex was about halfway done when it faced a major crisis. The European Union had just lowered the acceptable level of an impurity in the final product. The new regulation was more stringent than the processing facility was designed to produce. The inability to sell to a big region of the world would significantly reduce profits.

Once informed of the change, the project sponsor quickly organized all the groups involved in the new development—including the commercial group, the project team, the technology group, and the operations group—to develop a response to the problem. Without a

---

[1] I discuss the project sponsor and project manager relationship in more detail later in this chapter.
[2] This project was a megaproject, but the insight applies to any project, large or small.

project sponsor, the response would not have been as quick or effective. First, the job to respond would have fallen to the project manager. Second, given the project's size, the executive committee overseeing the project was the company's board of directors (BOD). Imagine trying to organize a series of meetings with the BOD to figure out what to do. Third, because the commercial group and operations leader representative did not report to the project manager, he would have struggled to get other stakeholders to adjust their priorities to fix this problem. You need one person who is focused on getting the entire venture back on track when a problem this major occurs. Even if the problem had been within the span of the project director's control, the project sponsor would need to communicate to the board of directors and potentially secure their approval to the response.

## Who Is the Project Sponsor?

We often think of the project sponsor as the person who "wants" the project. For example, an executive spots an opportunity and spearheads the effort to develop the full venture, including the capital project. This executive has the vision of how best to exploit the opportunity and can best lead the effort to make the vision a reality. Another scenario is that an executive or team of executives identifies an opportunity and assigns a project sponsor, often a lower-level executive, to act on their behalf. In this case, with the assignment, the project sponsor becomes the leading advocate for the project and takes on the accountability to deliver value from the opportunity (see Figure 4.2).

Under either scenario, the project sponsor operates under a mandate from higher-level executives unless the project sponsor is also the owner of the company. The project sponsor answers to a more senior executive or a team of executives who are responsible for the capital invested in the opportunity. They are tasked with protecting the interests of shareholders. They ensure that the capital invested is

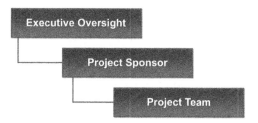

**Figure 4.2  Key Project Sponsor Relationships**

aligned with corporate and business strategy and that the investment
will provide a suitable return. I will describe the mandate in more
detail later, but basically it establishes the limits to the opportunity to
be pursued and the limits to the project sponsor's authority.

A study I did showed that many companies struggle with getting
the project sponsor role right and suffer the consequences of the lack of
a project sponsor. Only 60 percent of IPA clients actually had a clearly
defined role for a project sponsor assigned during the Assess stage of a
project. The remaining 40 percent either had no defined role or had
some vague description for the role. (See Figure 4.3.) The main reason
these companies lacked a strong project sponsor was that senior
management did not understand the project sponsor's role in project
governance.

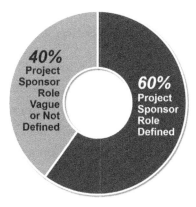

**Figure 4.3  Many Companies Do Not Define the Project Sponsor
Roles and Responsibilities**

Without a project sponsor, the average quality of the initial business case prepared at the end of the Assess stage was much worse than when there was a sponsor. A business case can be weak for any number of reasons. In Chapter 3, I showed that the business cases for 3 out of 10 projects were based on incomplete market analyses, which usually means the potential profit from the opportunity is overstated. A business case can also be weak because the capital cost and schedule estimate was just thrown together or the risk analysis misses a whole set of opportunities or threats to the project. It is certainly possible to develop a strong business case without a project sponsor. It just does not happen consistently unless there is one person who is accountable for the quality of the work.

## Overview of Project Sponsor Role

The project sponsor has three critical responsibilities in a project:

- Drives the development of a robust business case.
- Acts decisively to clear barriers or to fix problems that threaten the expected business value.
- Ensures that all work outside the remit of the project manager needed to reap the value from a project is completed.

The extent of the project sponsor responsibilities in each of these categories will vary according to the project and the resources a business has to support the project sponsor. For example, a project that opens up a new business area or region will most likely have a full-time sponsor who actively oversees work on the project, commercial negotiations, and the development of the business and asset operating organization. A project sponsor for a project making a small modification to an existing asset may only need a couple of hours a week. It just depends.

## Assign a Project Sponsor as the Initial Business Case Is Developed

The project sponsor position is assigned during the Assess stage of the project. Some companies assign the project sponsor right at the start as the project frame is developed. The advantage in this case is that the sponsor takes ownership right away. Others wait until the project frame is well under way before assigning the project sponsor. The advantage of this strategy is that you do not waste someone's time if the opportunity is found to be unattractive.

Choosing the project sponsor is usually not an easy task. Ideally, the project sponsor is the person who has the most at stake in achieving the business objectives when the project is complete. The ideal aligns a project sponsor's self-interest with the shareholders' self-interest to get the most value from the capital. If the project goal is to increase profits from additional sales, the business executive who is going to make money from selling the product would be a good candidate for the position. Sometimes compromises are required, however, because the best candidate is not available. Those compromises might include choosing someone with less experience or someone with less credibility or seniority in the organization. In this case, the person chosen might need additional training and/or mentorship from another executive in the company. I finish the chapter with some guidance on the knowledge and skills that project sponsors need to be effective.

## Requirements for a Strong Project Sponsor

These are the basic requirements that create a strong project sponsor position:

- The project sponsor owns the business case.
- Executives establish the mandate of the project sponsor.
- The project sponsor is held accountable at stage-gates.

## Make the Project Sponsor Own the Business Case

Here is a good first test for understanding the condition of project sponsorship at your company. Who presents the business case for stage-gate approval? The project sponsor owns the business case and should therefore be able to describe its contents thoroughly. If someone else has to make the presentation, it probably means that the project sponsor lacks a deep understanding of the project. Nothing will force a better understanding of the business case than the need to present the strengths and weaknesses of the business case and defend the decisions that shaped its contents. The project sponsor is responsible for preparing the contents of the business case but much of the work is delegated to others. For example, the project sponsor may not prepare the marketing forecast used to justify the expansion of a production facility, but he better make sure that the marketing forecast was done rigorously. Making the project sponsor own the business case also heads off the problem of the project sponsor blaming others for lapses or mistakes, such as missed deadlines or a poor-quality business case.

The purpose of this next example is to better describe what owning the business case really means. The project is called Flash. Project Flash is going to purchase and install new machinery at an existing manufacturing facility to improve the quality of a fabric used to make clothes. The material will be more durable but not at the sacrifice of softness or breathability. The business anticipates that the improved product quality will allow for increased sales and prices. A high-level summary of the initial business case is shown next. As you can see in Table 4.1, the business expects to make a nice return on investment, and, although there are some risks, the executives approved the project to move to the Select stage.

The project sponsor for this project was the global product manager and reported directly to the global business manager, who was ultimately responsible for the capital the company invests in

## Table 4.1  Initial Business Case for Project Flash

| | |
|---|---|
| Project Justification | • Increase profits in existing markets by providing improved and more cost-effective products. |
| Project Description | • Purchase and install a new finishing machine. |
| Business Objectives | • Exceed 25 percent internal rate of return. |
| | • Achieve unit cost of production of $0.14 per square meter. |
| | • Provide platform for future R&D product testing. |
| | • Startup in 15 months to beat competition to market. |
| Base Case Asset Capability | • To satisfy business objectives, the machine will have the following capability: |
| | – Production rate for five shifts/week: 10 million square meters |
| | – No more than 5 percent wasted product |
| | – Machine reliability is 95 percent run time |
| Project Scope | • Expand existing production building. |
| | • Upgrade utilities and storage. |
| | • Install new machinery. |
| Options to Evaluate in Select Stage | • Option to add 25% more capacity than base case. |
| | • Evaluate different machinery vendors. |
| Project Estimated Cost and Schedule | • Total capital is $30 million. Startup in 15 months. |
| Primary Risks to Business Success | • Customer acceptance of new product features. |
| | • Completion of customer qualification tests in time for startup. |
| | • Getting uniform product quality from new machine. |

the business unit. She was chosen because she will be leading the effort to sell the new products. She was assigned when the project frame was about halfway complete. At that time, executives had endorsed the opportunity and established preliminary objectives. The project sponsor's job was to complete the initial business case by finalizing the targets for the business objectives, making a decision on the options to be evaluated in the next stage, and overseeing the economic analysis used to justify the project. Most of the work was done by a small team of engineering resources needed to develop the conceptual scope for the project. The project sponsor spent about 20 percent of her time leading the project frame and the development of the initial business case. That level of effort continued to about halfway through the Select stage when the final options were selected. The sponsor's effort then dropped to about 10 percent for the remainder of the project.

The project sponsor's leadership was critical to getting a robust business case. In particular, the project sponsor had to make a series of important decisions about the business objectives and priorities between different targets. I am going to describe two decisions that were made to provide a sense of the project sponsor role.

The project sponsor had to make a trade-off decision between how long it would be before the business could provide samples to the customer for product qualification and the amount of time the technology group would have for testing the new machinery. Customers for the improved fabric require samples for performance testing before they agree to buy the product. The technology group wanted to add one month to do some additional testing before finalizing the design to reduce the technical risk of inconsistent product quality. One month more of testing meant a one-month delay in getting product samples for customer qualification. In the end, the project sponsor, with the recommendation of the project team, allowed the additional testing.

Another issue that had to be worked through was the strategic objective to provide R&D with the ability to use the new machine for product development for other business units that made different types of fabrics. Adding the capability was the right thing for the company but did not provide much benefit to the business unit sponsoring the project. The project sponsor had to work with her counterpart in the other business unit to reach an agreement on the scope of work for this objective.

## Establish the Mandate for the Project Sponsor

A project sponsor, of course, is not free to do anything she wants. She cannot pursue an opportunity or set business objectives that are not aligned with corporate and business strategy. By providing a clear set of boundary conditions and givens, executives establish the limits to the project sponsor role. For example, one of the boundary conditions for this project was to specify the location of the project. The company has two locations that manufacture the product. The global business manager, however, wanted the project done at one location.

You have to be careful that the boundary conditions are not overly tight so that you place too many constraints on the project sponsor. The project frame or other project documentation like a project charter are your tools for being clear about what decisions you want to make and what decisions the project sponsor is allowed to make. The executives continue to keep tabs on the project sponsor through regular progress reports or meetings to update status.

## Hold Project Sponsors Accountable at the Stage-Gates

Once you establish clear expectations for the project sponsor role, you have to hold them accountable for their work to get the performance you want. Being held accountable for your actions is the mechanism for getting people to behave according to expectations. Usually we think about the negative when we discuss accountability. Basically, someone gets in trouble if things do not go well. The fear of punishment causes people to worry about the results of their actions and, in doing so, causes them to perform better. The knowledge that I am accountable for the safety of others while driving my car causes me to drive better. However, accountability also means that good performance is rewarded. Doing the project sponsor job well often requires personal sacrifice because of the time requirements, and it often means performing a role that they are not well trained for. Without the potential for reward, you have a job that is hard and only gets recognized if something negative occurs. People will scramble out of their offices when they see you coming rather than saying, *Sign me up chief!*

Using business outcomes only to judge project sponsor performance is a weak accountability mechanism. For instance, you could say a project sponsor was successful if a project that was expected to deliver $5 million in NPV delivered at least that amount or more. Also, you could say a project sponsor was not successful if a project that promised to deliver $5 million in NPV only delivered $2 million. You may or may not be right. A project may have succeeded despite the fact that the project sponsor failed—or may have failed even if the project sponsor did everything right. For example, many of the projects that were completed just as the global financial crisis hit in 2008 did not make as much money as expected because of the economic downturn. It would be unreasonable to say the project sponsor should have foreseen the crisis that very few saw coming. The difficulty is that you do not know unless there is some analysis after a project is complete *why* a project succeeded or failed, not just that it did or did not.

Some companies use investment lookbacks to assess project sponsor performance. The lookback is usually conducted one or two years after the project is complete to compare the actual value delivered to what was expected when the project was funded and to identify the reasons for the result. To make this work, the company must have the discipline to conduct the lookbacks routinely and do the analysis thoroughly every time. The discipline is needed because linking project sponsor decisions to results can be difficult. For major investments, several years can pass between the time the project sponsor is most active and the realization of value. Many things outside the project sponsor's control can contribute to the success or failure of the project. The analysis has to be rigorous enough to identify the project sponsor's contribution.

There is also a good chance that the project sponsor at the start of the project will not be there when it is over. As I explain at the end of this chapter, half of all projects have a change in the project sponsor position during the project's life span. It is harder to hold someone accountable after the sponsor has moved on to another position because she may not suffer the consequences of bad results. For example, an unprofitable project may burden the financial performance of a business for many years, thereby lowering the bonuses of the executives running the business during that period. A project sponsor that has moved on to a new job will not suffer financially unless the company establishes a system to dock her variable compensation no matter what role she has in the company.

The most effective mechanism for holding project sponsors accountable is to judge the completeness of the business case they present at the stage-gate and to have consequences if the quality is poor. The most immediate consequence is that a project does not make it through the stage-gate if the quality of the business case does not meet expectations. You can be assured that stopping a project at a gate will get everyone's attention.

Holding project sponsors accountable at the stage-gate also protects the business. You really do not want to wait until a project is over before having an idea of how well the project sponsor did. You would rather not figure out that the business case used to justify a project was a house of cards *after* wasting a good chunk of shareholder capital. It would be better to head off disasters before they occur.

For each stage-gate, a business establishes the minimum requirements for the work used to develop the business case. The requirements are not an accident. The requirements are based on the information that business needs to make a good investment decision at each stage-gate. The business case should meet all the requirements. There can be exceptions, of course. Sometimes a requirement cannot be met, and there is a compelling business reason for allowing the project to move forward. For instance, a business may have a requirement that the contract for supplying feedstock for new production has to be signed before senior management will approve the project. The cost of the feedstock has such a large impact on the project economics that they are not willing to take the risk that the cost will be significantly higher than the amount used in the investment analysis. However, a project sponsor who is having difficultly completing negotiations with a supplier might make a case that the chances of higher costs are low and delaying the project is unnecessary. The project sponsor must seek permission and provide sound justification for allowing an exception to the business requirement. Ultimately, it is the executives making the stage-gate decision who decide whether the exception is warranted, not the project sponsor.

## Focus on the Project Sponsor Behaviors That Produce Robust Business Cases

A key role of the project sponsor is to balance the competing interests of the business and primary stakeholders. You want them to drive for maximum value, while staying within the boundary conditions of the business case and keeping risks at an acceptable level. This is a tough task and can only be accomplished if there is mutual respect between the people involved in the project because there will be conflict. People will inevitably disagree on what is needed to make a project successful. If the relationships are weak, the conflict will allow problems to fester or cause good ideas to be withheld. This is a list of behaviors that you want the project sponsor to exhibit to create the environment needed for success:

- Fosters an atmosphere of trust and open communication with the project manager and the rest of the project team.

- Acts decisively and takes responsibility for their decisions.

- Challenges the project team to find ways to maximize value, including a push to explore meaningful alternatives.

- Seeks input and consensus on the contents of the business case with executives.

- Engages peers in the organization for advice and support for key decisions.

- Reviews and responds to results of independent reviews of the project.

## Building a Strong Project Sponsor and Project Manager Relationship

The most important relationship is between the project sponsor and the project manager. Neither can succeed without the other. The project sponsor is accountable for delivering the value from the project. The project manager is accountable for delivering an asset that meets specifications in a set time frame and within a certain budget. If the project manager fails, the project sponsor will not be able to deliver the expected value. However, the project manager is also highly dependent on the project sponsor. If the project sponsor sets targets for cost and schedule that have a high level of risk, the project manager may be doomed to fail.

Project outcomes are likely to be poor when project sponsors take a my-way-or-the-highway approach to project development. They set aggressive targets and shout down the concerns from the project manager about meeting those targets. Here is an example of a project sponsor whose approach led to a project disaster. The business makes an ingredient that is used by food companies to improve the nutritional value of their products. Over the years, the business had made incremental improvements to its production process around the world by making small upgrades here and there. The business strategy for a project was to build a brand-new line using the best of the best from the existing production lines to build a very efficient production line. The technical challenge was that design was not easy and would take some time to do right. The business challenge was that the project sponsor was insisting on a project schedule that was about six months too short to do all the technical work needed to bring all the pieces together. As is often the case, the project's financial return was dependent on meeting a calendar date. The project sponsor needed to have the additional product available during the period the food companies would make their purchasing decisions for the coming year. The food companies would base their purchase of the food ingredient on their sales forecasts for the next 12 months. The conflict was that the project sponsor was insisting on setting the schedule to meet the calendar date despite the project team's feedback that the date was infeasible. In the end, the project sponsor pushed the project through without acknowledging the technical risk. The risk came back and bit the business. The team was not able to meet the schedule target, the market window was missed, and money spent trying to go fast was wasted.

The steps to building a strong relationship between the project sponsor and project manager begin as soon as the project manager is assigned. As discussed earlier, the project sponsor is assigned sometime during the Assess stage of the project. Ideally, the project manager is also named as the initial business case is being completed. Unless the project is very large, the project manager job is probably not full time during the Assess stage, as the work is still being led within the organization sponsoring the project. However, the project manager can provide valuable input on the strengths and weaknesses of project strategies that are being considered for the project during the Assess stage. In particular, input from the project manager can help avoid the problem of setting impossible targets at the start of the project. Also, early involvement gives the project manager a better understanding of the project and the business objectives, which allows them to hit the ground running as they begin to develop the project team, usually at the start of the Select stage.

## Choosing the Right Project Sponsor

The executive with overall responsibility for the capital usually has the lead in assigning the project sponsor. As mentioned earlier, the perfect candidate may not be available. Not only does the ideal person need to be experienced and have a diverse set of skills, he or she also has to be available at the right time. Because the timing of capital projects is difficult to predict, there is a good chance the best candidate has another important assignment. There are ways to compensate for a few weaknesses. For example, say the person you assign has never been involved in capital projects before. That is not ideal, but you can team them up with a very experienced project director or project manager who can coach them in certain areas. What is important is that a project manager with expertise and complementary skills is put in place to compensate.

Here are some important criteria to consider when choosing a project sponsor:

- Seniority and credibility
- Knowledge of the business and its operations

- Interpersonal and critical thinking skills
- Understanding of basic project management concepts
- Continuity

## Seniority and Credibility

Capital projects go much better when there is internal consensus, especially at the management level, that a project is addressing a real business need and that the project scope and strategy are well matched with the business goals. The project sponsor is responsible for communicating the need for the project, explaining the logic behind important decisions, and convincing key individuals, including functional groups, to support the project.

Take, for example, a project in which the sales department wants to purchase new customer relationship management software. The sales department wants software that is easier to use and provides more insight on which marketing channels are paying off. The project sponsor appointed to the project must have enough seniority and credibility to get the internal stakeholders aligned on the project. The IT department will be involved in the selection of the software. The department will ask questions like: *Is it compatible with our existing hardware? What is the software vendor's history of providing customer support?* The project sponsor must be high enough in the sales organization to engage the IT department and make sure the selection process gives proper weight to the user benefits from the software rather than just focusing on the difficulty of maintaining the system. The project sponsor must be able to get regional sales managers to buy into the new system and support its rollout. Perhaps the CEO will ask for a presentation to explain why the company is spending a few million dollars on a new system. The project sponsor must be credible and knowledgeable when making the presentation to gain the CEO's support.

The project sponsor is also the external face of the project. Large capital projects can have interfaces with partners, suppliers, governments, and local communities. Disagreements with these stakeholders about the project can easily derail the venture. The project sponsor's negotiation skills here are critical. Agreements with key stakeholders are forged from negotiations about what the stakeholder will get out of the project. Partners want a share of the profits based on their contribution to the project. Suppliers negotiate based on the price for their goods and services. Governments and local communities will support a project based on tax revenues, jobs created, and other benefits. The project sponsor must reach agreements with external stakeholders but not negotiate away so much value that the project is no longer profitable for the business. The sponsor must have enough seniority to assure external stakeholders that they are actually working with someone with decision-making authority. The project sponsor does not have to personally negotiate every deal or engage with every stakeholder. Some of the requirements can be delegated to the project manager or others when appropriate.

## Knowledge of the Business and Its Operations

Understanding the business is usually the easiest criterion to meet because the project sponsor is typically from the business or organization doing the project. The project sponsor needs to understand how the business will make money with the asset and how the asset will operate to produce products or services.

## Interpersonal and Critical Thinking Skills

The nature of the project sponsor role and the project sponsor's high level of interaction with internal and external stakeholders demands that the sponsor have strong interpersonal skills. Critical thinking skills, including the ability to work with ambiguity, are important.

Take a project that is adding production capacity. One option is to add 50 percent more capacity using tried and true technology. Another option is to use a new technology that will add 100 percent (double) to existing capacity at the same price. But, there is a one in four chance the new technology will not work. Which do you want? The project sponsor must be able to work through the decision-making process with the project team to answer the question. In addition, other attributes that should describe the project sponsor include ability to see the *big picture*, excellent communication and listening skills, ability to collaborate, and openness to learning.

## Understanding of Basic Project Management Concepts

If the knowledge of business is the easiest criterion to meet, understanding project management is usually the hardest. Project management is the application of knowledge, skills, tools, and techniques to achieve objectives. The discipline includes a host of concepts, including team organization, project definition, risk management, project controls, and change management. In my experience, most project sponsors have never been part of a capital project before, or if they have, it may have been so long ago that they do not remember much.

Nobody should expect or even want project sponsors to be project management experts. It is not their job. The problem, and the opportunity, is that the actions of the project sponsor have a huge impact on the project leader's ability to apply these concepts. For example, a project sponsor who does not give clear instructions on project priorities makes it more difficult to develop robust project strategies. In fact, there are so many interdependencies between the project sponsor and the project manager that it can be very difficult to know, when something goes wrong, whether the source of the problem was the project sponsor or the project manager or both.

The majority of this book is intended to give project sponsors (and executives) the basics of what they need to know to be effective. Companies that routinely do capital projects will deliver internal training programs to provide a background on the concepts.

## Continuity

The track record of IPA's clients maintaining continuity of project sponsors on major capital investments in industry is terrible. Approximately half of the major projects in IPA's database will turn over the project sponsor sometime during the life of the project. Changing the project sponsor during that period usually results in at least 5 percent cost growth, adds 11 percent to the project life cycle, and lowers asset technical performance by 15 percent. That is a huge penalty to pay for turnover (see Figure 4.4). The new project sponsor is likely to have other priorities or ideas for the project objectives. If nothing else, do not change the project sponsor and the project manager at the same time.

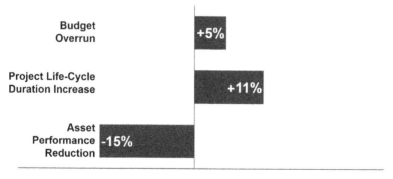

**Figure 4.4  Project Sponsor Turnover Can Destroy Value**

# 5 The Single Most Important Thing an Executive Can Do to Make Any Capital Project Succeed

## Define Clear Objectives

I f you want your capital projects to succeed, this is the area you should focus on. Get this activity right and you will avoid many of the problems that occur later in a project's life cycle.

In Chapter 2, I said that a goal of the Assess stage is to answer the question: *What is the best way to take advantage of an opportunity or to solve a problem that will maximize value?* Clear objectives identify the criteria that guide the work to select the option that will likely maximize value.

Most executives involved in making key decisions on capital projects fail at this step. Only one in three project teams report that they fully understand the project's objectives as they begin their work. Not having clear objectives has real consequences. Projects without clear objectives are 50 percent more likely to have a major change or recycle later in the project life cycle, which leads to delays and higher costs. On average, you will spend 10 percent more capital because of the inefficiencies created by unclear objectives. You are also much more likely to have a disaster project that erodes more than half the value that was expected to be created.

The "bring me a rock" story is often used to describe the problem of unclear objectives. One version of the story goes something like this:

> Your boss asks you to bring him a rock. Being a good employee you run outside to find a rock and bring it back to your boss. Your boss looks at the rock and says, "That is not the right rock. I need a bigger, rounder rock." You go outside again and find a rock you think matches the description. You bring it back and your boss says, "You are getting closer, but the rock needs to be a blue rock." This goes on and on until you bring your boss a rock that matches his need.

Considerable time and effort would have been avoided if your boss had just given you all the criteria he was using to decide whether you brought the right rock in the first place. A project I reviewed is a perfect example of the consequences of not being clear about objectives. The project was delayed six months to redo the engineering design simply because it was never made clear what the business executives wanted at the start of the project. The project was not complex. The business just needed a small expansion of an existing plant and commissioned a project team to start work. They wanted the extra capacity at the lowest possible capital cost to get them by for the next couple of years. Demand for the product was uncertain over the long term, and they wanted to minimize fixed costs. While doing the initial design, the engineers responsible for the process took the opportunity to make some upgrades to allow the plant to run more efficiently and to lower variable costs. Of course, the upgrades added to the cost of the project. When the project team presented the cost estimate to the business executives for approval, the executives rejected the improvements the engineers had made. The cost was more than they wanted to spend. The business priority was to minimize capital cost because of the market uncertainty. They did not want to invest additional capital even if it lowered variable production costs. The problem would have been avoided if there had just been some basic communication about objectives before the project was handed over to the project team. This problem is relatively easy to fix.

Sometimes the problem is more complicated. Sometimes the boss does not even know what type of rock he needs because of the complexity of the problem. The boss cannot describe it because many objectives have to be satisfied and choosing the right rock is not obvious. Rather than attempting to describe the rock, the boss should list all his objectives and let you do the work to figure out which is the right rock. If the objectives are not comprehensive, you may still end up bringing your boss the wrong rock.

In this chapter, I am going to describe how to develop clear objectives for either situation to help you avoid falling into the trap of *bring me a rock*.

## Business Objectives versus Project Objectives

Before getting started, I want to be up front that I am lumping together business objectives and project objectives. Business objectives describe the reason a business wants to do a project. Project objectives are the means for achieving the business objectives. For example, a statement like this includes a business objective and a project objective: *lower operating costs (business objective) by installing a new technology (project objective)*. Also, I am not going to focus on the difference between targets and constraints. A target is what a business wants to accomplish; a constraint is something that cannot be violated to have a viable business case. These distinctions would be important if I were trying to explain how to structure objectives to drive good project decision making. My goal is simply to make you aware of the need for comprehensive objectives to ensure all the criteria that will be used to select options and to make other choices on project scope and strategy are established.[1]

## Developing Clear Objectives

There are three basic sources of unclear objectives:

1. Objectives are not comprehensive—usually because the project frame is not complete.
2. The project team does not understand the objectives.
3. The trade-offs between objectives are not prioritized.

---

[1]This book does an excellent job explaining the process for structuring objectives to support project decision making: Reidar B. Bratvold and Steve H. Begg, *Making Good Decisions* (Richardson, TX: Society of Petroleum Engineers, 2010).

**Table 5.1  Example of Objectives**

| Objective | Target or Minimum Requirement |
|---|---|
| 1. Return on Investment | At least 30 percent IRR |
| 2. Operating Cost Reduction | Reduce by $9/ton |
| 3. Capital Cost per Unit of Production | Below $400/ton |
| 4. Capital Cost Target | No more than $100 million |
| 5. Start of Production | Approximately 36 months |

## Developing Comprehensive Objectives

A weak project frame leaves out key objectives or the boundary conditions that constrain the objective. Missing objectives may mean that some of the options that could potentially deliver a higher level of value may be missed or that the options investigated will, in the end, be unworkable. Here is a short example of how a comprehensive set of objectives guides the identification and selection of options.

Table 5.1 shows a set of objectives developed for a project that will expand production capacity.[2] A business forecasted 8 to 9 percent growth over the next 10 years for one of its main products. The business objectives were to increase profits and to defend market share. Defending market share was important. The business had a volume leadership position that resulted in a significant product cost advantage over its competitors. Executives commissioned a project frame to investigate the opportunity and define the target condition. Eventually, the target condition developed from the project frame was to expand capacity by 300 kilotons per annum by a series of incremental expansions of its existing facility. The target condition and the associated objectives were developed within the context of business

---

[2]For simplicity, I am not including objectives for health and safety performance and other social responsibility requirements that would certainly be included as fundamental objectives for a project like this.

strategy, possible competitor actions, and understanding of the business's current assets. For example, an option rejected early on was building a new, stand-alone facility. That option was in conflict with the business's strategy to build a new plant in another region, and there was a risk that competitors would build additional capacity and try to take market share by cutting prices.

The important information shown in the table is (1) there are multiple objectives that have to be met to have a viable business case and to maximize the value from the investment, and (2) each of the objectives had a performance measure that was either a target or constraint for the objective. For example, the project's return on investment has to be at least 30 percent to be economically viable. The goal for operating cost reduction is a target. The business wants to improve its cost advantage even further by reducing operating costs. The reduction of $9 per ton represents a target executives think is achievable. They have included the target to guide the identification and selection of options, but they will not know whether the target can be achieved until further analysis is done.

Using these criteria, eight different options for incremental expansion were identified. Some initial economic and technical analysis performed on the options winnowed the list down to four potential options. Two of the options met all the objectives, including the hurdle rate for return on investment. The initial business case was completed, and plans were developed to further investigate the four options in the Select stage. The project would be susceptible to falling into the bring-me-a-rock trap if any of these objectives were missing or did not have a target or constraint.

## Confirm Alignment of Objectives with Business and Corporate Strategy

Executives can run into trouble if the objectives are not aligned with business or corporate strategy. In the previous example, the decision not to build a new plant was a boundary condition because of business strategy. If the boundary conditions were not included, the executives may have pursued an option that just would have been eliminated later.

Alignment with corporate strategies is also critical for establishing clear objectives. For example, a company may have a corporate strategy for using a common manufacturing platform across all its business units. The common platform uses standard pieces of equipment to make all of the company's core products. By standardizing, the company can deploy new technology more effectively, leverage development costs, and shorten the project schedule by eliminating the time needed to design the process. The trade-off with a common platform is that sometimes its application may not be optimal for a particular project. In some cases, the equipment will provide more capability than the business needs. In other cases, the equipment may not be able to meet all the customers' specifications.

In my experience, executives sponsoring projects will push to deviate from corporate strategies when the strategy has a negative effect on their specific project. Using the common platform example, the project sponsor may push for a fit-for-purpose design rather going with the standard design. The push represents the tug of war between the drive to maximize the value from individual capital projects and corporate strategies that are designed to maximize the value from a portfolio of projects. Corporate executives need to be involved and provide input to a project frame to ensure corporate strategies are captured as boundary conditions or give explicit approval of the deviation.

## Surface Strategic Objectives Early

Another challenge to developing clear objectives is working within strategic objectives. Some capital projects are critical for building capability that positions a business for long-term success. Examples of strategic objectives advanced through capital projects include things like:

- Proving a new product or manufacturing technology
- Establishing a base of operations in a new location
- Strengthening a key customer relationship to become a preferred supplier

The rub with strategic objectives is that there is often a trade-off with the business objective to maximize the financial return. For example, a project to establish a base of operations in a new country can be long, costly, and risky as the business learns the requirements for the new area. However, the strategic value of the objective is that the new base of operations could be used to launch a series of profitable projects in the future. Executives have to decide whether the near-term cost is worth the potential long-term opportunity.[3]

Surfacing strategic objectives allows their merits to be debated and the cost estimates to be developed to support a deliberate decision on how much economic value the business is willing to trade for long-term value. Without the debate, a project may move away from the strategic objective because of pressure to increase financial value. Some executives may not even be aware of the strategic objective. The long-term benefit of proving a new technology in a project may only be known by the technology executive, for instance.

---

[3]One method the financial community sometimes uses to assess the value of strategic objectives like this is called Real Options Analysis. In this case, the analysis assigns a value to having the ability to expand the new base of operations in the future. Although much is written about this technique, my observation is that even IPA's clients, who are among the most sophisticated in their approach to investment analysis, do not routinely use the method. The more common approach is to list the strategic objective as a fundamental objective so that its importance stays front and center.

Early identification can also prevent the problem of the strategic objective from becoming the sole reason for doing the project. You have probably been in an investment committee meeting in which the project sponsor is arguing passionately that the strategic goals of a project justify approval even though the numbers do not look that good. The project sponsor might say, "Meeting client requirements on this project will make us a preferred supplier in the future. The client wants a commitment now or they will look for someone else." The project sponsor's assertion may be entirely correct, but the investment committee meeting where the funding decision is made should not be the first time you and other executives are learning about it, and the assertion has to be defended by a compelling explanation, supported by data, that shows how the value will be realized in the future.

## Communicating the Objectives

You can do a fantastic job defining objectives in the Assess stage but still fail to have clear objectives if the project team does not understand them. At some point during the Select stage, usually near the start, primary responsibility for a project transfers from the organization sponsoring the project to a project manager and a project team. As I discussed earlier, the business unit or any organization sponsoring a project is responsible for developing the project frame and preparing the initial business case for the Assess stage-gate. A project manager and project team are needed to take that initial work and start project definition. The project team must have a very good understanding of what you want to guide their decision making as they do their work.

My first example of the project team that did not know that the business's primary priority was low capital cost was a particularly egregious example of miscommunication. Oftentimes, the misunderstanding is more subtle, but it still leads to a lower return on investment from a project. I will describe how to communicate objectives, but first I will give an example of the benefit from effective communication of objectives and the underlying business case to the project team. Project teams can help you develop project objectives that enable you to capture the upside in the uncertainty while protecting against the downside, but they can only do this if you share the uncertainty underlying the business objectives.

## Communicate the Uncertainty in the Business Case to Get Better Project Objectives

Business cases are often built on forecasts that contain considerable uncertainty. Some examples of uncertainty include the introduction of new products that do not have an established market or the deployment of technology that is not proved. Consumers could embrace the new product or react with indifference. The new technology could perform wonderfully, or it could be a total disaster. A classic dilemma faced by business is what size asset to build when demand is uncertain. For a new product, it is difficult for business to pin down how many customers will want to purchase the product until it is available. The company could build a small plant and expand it later if the demand is at the high end of the range rather than building a large plant immediately. But building a small plant trades protection from wasted capital if demand is low for lost profits if demand is high.

Communicating the uncertainty in demand gives the project team some very clear instructions. The project team knows it needs to estimate the cost differences between the large plant and small plant as well as the time needed to expand if the small plant is built. The information, however, may not be readily available, and the team will need some time and money to obtain it. You need to allow enough time and be willing to pay for the work to generate the estimates. Also, the project team may come up with better options you did not even think were possible. For example, there may be an option to build a large plant while minimizing fixed costs, or perhaps the team can design the small plant in a way that allows the expansion to be done faster. The project team can only present you with creative, valuable options when they know the uncertainty exists *and* when they understand which strategies will help capture upside while controlling risk.

## Explain the Objectives Face-to-Face

There is no magic formula to explain the objectives to the project team. It just involves face-to-face communication, usually done in workshops with structured agendas, wherein the project sponsor and other executives talk about the project with the project team. The project team is encouraged to openly question and discuss issues so that risks and uncertainties, tasks, and priorities are fully understood throughout the project team.[4] It is so easy for teams to misunderstand what is expected of them unless there is an opportunity for an open discussion about the project. As I will explain in more detail shortly, the best way to avoid misunderstandings is to force a very specific discussion about trade-offs between objectives and the executive's priorities when trade-offs are required. Open discussion will also highlight areas where objectives are vague because there is no performance measure assigned to the objective. An objective that states "lower operating costs" is relatively meaningless until a value is assigned like "by 20 percent."

---

[4]I used the word *encouraged* in this sentence on purpose. The project sponsor and other executives usually have more seniority than the project manager and the other project team members. They may not feel comfortable challenging the executives about the project, the likelihood that the objectives will be achieved, or the robustness of the project strategies that have already been outlined.

### Executives Have to Show Up and Participate

Many IPA clients run workshops based on IPA research to facilitate the communication of objectives. Although these workshops are extremely effective at communicating objectives, it seems like executives view these workshops as the equivalent of going to the dentist because it can be impossible to get them to come. Actually, I think they probably go to the dentist more frequently. When they do appear, their participation can be superficial. The problem is especially acute when the project sponsor role has not been clearly defined. Without a clear project sponsor, there is no single person that is responsible for ensuring the communication takes place, and there is no one with the seniority to get other executives to participate. All executives who are key internal stakeholders need to provide timely input and engage in serious dialogue, so that the project team understands what you want.

## Prioritizing the Objectives

One reason establishing clear objectives is difficult is that capital projects have multiple objectives that have to be satisfied, and those objectives compete against one another, meaning improving performance in one area requires trading performance in another. Often there are difficult choices to be made. An easy personal example about making trade-offs is the process you go through when buying a car. When I go to buy a car, I start thinking of all the nice features I could get. More power, leather seats, a navigation system, a collision warning system, and a high quality sound system are all things I would like to have. When the cost for all those options is added up, the total may exceed what I want to spend. Of course, if money is no object, I do not need to make trade-offs. Most of us and most businesses, however, are not in the position where money is no object; therefore, trade-offs have to be made if all the features I want exceed my cost budget.

A trade-off means you have to give up one thing to get another. When buying this car, I might have to give up the deluxe leather seats and premium sound system to keep the total cost at or below my budget. I have to decide whether I want those features *or* whether I want to keep the cost below my budget. I cannot have both unless I cut something somewhere else or increase my budget. For me, I wrestle with trade-off decisions like these because I really want all the nice features *and* I want to keep the price below my budget. Also, there is the potential I will regret my decision later. For example, I may decide to cut some of the features I want, but then be very disappointed with the car later because it does not have those features.

Executives wrestle with trade-off decisions even more. Competition often makes it very difficult to develop projects that will deliver enough profit to justify the capital cost. If you ask executives whether they prefer a fast schedule *or* low cost, they might respond by saying they need a fast schedule *and* low cost; otherwise, there is no project. Unfortunately, sometimes the trade-off cannot be avoided. The executive has to accept the trade-off, try a different approach, or kill the project.

The workshops I described earlier can also help executives work through trade-off decisions. All key internal stakeholders attend the meeting so that they can express their preferences and debate particular choices. There are different ways of setting priorities, but, in general, the group makes choices in categories like those shown in Figure 5.1. There are more categories than I am showing here, and the categories can be tailored to the project, but these get the point across.

Let's do a quick example. Say the project sponsor chooses asset reliability of 95 to 99 percent as a high priority. This means she is willing to spend the money needed to design and build a highly reliable asset. There may be a problem if she also choses the lowest possible capital cost as a high priority. It may not be possible for the project team to design an asset that achieves high reliability at the

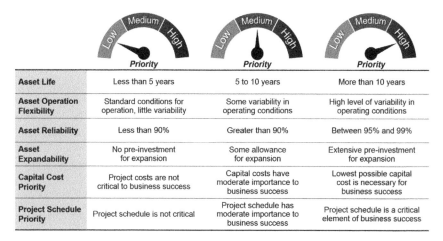

| | Priority | Priority | Priority |
|---|---|---|---|
| **Asset Life** | Less than 5 years | 5 to 10 years | More than 10 years |
| **Asset Operation Flexibility** | Standard conditions for operation, little variability | Some variability in operating conditions | High level of variability in operating conditions |
| **Asset Reliability** | Less than 90% | Greater than 90% | Between 95% and 99% |
| **Asset Expandability** | No pre-investment for expansion | Some allowance for expansion | Extensive pre-investment for expansion |
| **Capital Cost Priority** | Project costs are not critical to business success | Capital costs have moderate importance to business success | Lowest possible capital cost is necessary for business success |
| **Project Schedule Priority** | Project schedule is not critical | Project schedule has moderate importance to business success | Project schedule is a critical element of business success |

**Figure 5.1  Assigning the Relative Priority for Project Objectives**

lowest possible cost. Now, the project sponsor has to decide whether she wants high asset reliability *or* the lowest possible cost. Perhaps the resolution is that the project sponsor can accept greater than 90 percent reliability in order to save money, or maybe she is willing to spend more money to gain higher reliability. It may be that the project sponsor has to have both. In that case, something else has to give. Whether the project sponsor has to sacrifice asset reliability for a lower project cost will probably not be known until the costs are estimated for either option. Activities like these to set priorities almost always require further discussion, so that the project sponsor and other executives can decide what to do.

# 6 The Executive's Role in Building and Supporting High-Performing Project Teams

One question I asked executives while preparing to write this book was, "What can project teams do to better serve executives?" Perhaps there was some information or ways of interacting with the executives that would support better decision making or give them a more comprehensive understanding of the project's status. One person I asked was a project director with 30 years of experience and a strong track record of success. I had to pull the phone away from my ear when I asked him the question. He said (paraphrased), "Paul, what you need to explain in the book is how executives can better support project teams. They just do not understand how important their support is for success." Admittedly, he is strongly biased in his views, but he did have a very good point.

Executives can do a better job helping project teams succeed. The good news is that this support will not take much of your time, and will pay off many times over. Sometimes all the team needs is for you to pick up the phone and call one of your peers to get their organization to make a decision or to provide some information. For example, a project manager may come to you because the procurement group is late with a list of approved vendors for the project and does not appear to be giving the request much priority. In five minutes, your call to the procurement manager may get him to address the issue and allow your team to get its work done.

The executive in this chapter is primarily the project sponsor. In some cases, the project sponsor may have to go to a higher-level executive to get resources or have an issue addressed at a more senior level. Let's say a project is being done to upgrade a company's financial reporting software to a common system and platform across the company's multibusiness units. The project sponsor from corporate finance may need to work with each senior business executive to get them to supply the user representatives the project team needs.

## Executive Leaders Lead

A high-performing project team can make the work to deliver a successful project appear effortless. They are able to develop solutions and strategies that add value, complete their work on time, keep the project moving forward, and spot and correct any risks that threaten success before they have a chance to disrupt the project. In 2000, IPA began working on research to identify the ingredients of a high-performing team, so that it would be easier for clients to replicate the successful teams that produced better project results. We were able to develop a model and identify the attributes of successful teams. The attributes can be grouped into three main elements: (1) project leadership, (2) project development, and (3) team behavior (see Figure 6.1). Project teams that rated highly on all three elements tend to have more predictable results *and* provide better value for the money invested. Collectively, a strong team develops project strategies and designs that are less risky and more cost effective—all-in-all better solutions—and implements those solutions with greater care to head off problems and to produce superior results.

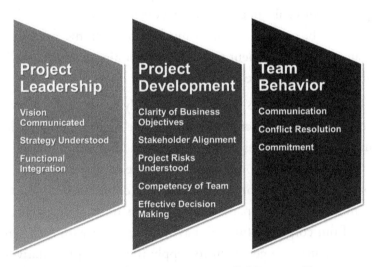

**Figure 6.1  Elements That Drive Successful Project Teams**

Project leadership, project development, and team behaviors work together like a three-legged stool. When one leg is weak, the whole effort is wobbly. The project manager bears the primary responsibility for building a high-performing team. The project manager selects the team members, organizes the team, communicates goals, establishes roles and responsibilities, and creates the environment that enables the team to work together to achieve the objectives. There are, however, several factors here that are the primary responsibility of the project sponsor or other executives. These factors include communicating the vision and strategy, defining and endorsing clear objectives, and ensuring the project team is functionally integrated.

Communicating the vision and strategy and translating both into clear objectives allow team members to make an emotional connection to the project and form the interpersonal relationships necessary for good teamwork. Clear objectives give people a goal to rally around and get team members to pull in the same direction. I know from working with many project teams that being on a project often means making personal sacrifices. A project is a perpetual set of deadlines (until it is finished); team members will work long hours and weekends when the work just has to get done. Projects often require relocation or extensive travel and time away from family to select and manage the work of suppliers and contractors. Our research shows that people are more likely to commit to making a project successful if they understand the objectives and why achieving those objectives is important to the business. Executives—not project managers—establish objectives. Project managers work with the executives to clarify and deepen the objectives. Project managers communicate objectives to the project team, but they cannot create them without your guidance.

Executives/sponsors need to stay in touch with the project team. It is not enough to come in and out of the project when requested. Keeping current can be done via a combination of visits, periodic updates, individual updates, and steering committee meetings. This becomes even more important for very large and/or remote projects.

## Invest in a Strong Owner Project Team

The owner project team gathers all the functions needed to develop and oversee the execution of a capital project. The role of the owner team is twofold. First, the owner team brings together the business expertise to fashion a project scope and strategy that will build or sustain a competitive advantage for a business. Let's say a project is going to upgrade the services offered to customers via a new web interface. The sales people who understand how customers will use the new website and what will make for a better customer experience must be on the team to help design the website. They know what customers want; their expertise has to be built into the project. Second, the owner team protects the best interests of the business by monitoring the activities of all third-party suppliers. Owner personnel take corrective action or raise an alarm as early as possible to head off trouble.

The project manager builds the owner project team. But, as the executive, you pay the bill. The project manager is responsible for identifying what skills are required, when each skill needs to be present, and the number of people needed in each position on the owner team. The project manager then brings you the proposal for discussion. In my experience, your first reaction may be, "Why do you need so many people?" Really what you mean is, "How can it cost that much?" The owner team is expensive, ranging from 3 to 11 percent of the total project cost just for the salaries, overhead costs, and fringe benefits for the people on the team.[1] That cost is a tempting target for

---

[1] I am showing a broad range for the cost of the owner team because the size required depends on a host of factors, including the type of project being done, the project's complexity, the contracting and procurement strategy used, and the experience and capability of the team members.

"savings," especially on projects that have marginal business cases. Some of the biggest disagreements I have witnessed between the executives and project managers are over the cost of the owner project team. The project manager usually argues for more resources and the executives argue the opposite.

Robust owner teams produce capital assets that are higher quality and less expensive than owner teams that are understaffed or that have outsourced much of the owner team role to contractors. IPA can benchmark the number of owner personnel a project team needs based on a number of factors, including project size, project team structure, and contracting strategy. Capital projects with understaffed owner project teams relative to the benchmarks cost more than adequately staffed projects by about 7 percent. In other words, if a project done with an understaffed owner team costs $100 million, that same project would cost approximately $93.5 million *even after* including the cost for the extra staff. Part of the savings is because the owner team finds ways of doing the project better. Well-staffed project teams are more likely to develop efficient designs and project strategies. Well-staffed owner teams also are better at controlling project risk. IPA routinely reviews projects that have cost growth and schedule slip because the team is unable to stay on top of the project. IPA recently reviewed a project that was expected to overrun by more than 15 percent just because the owner team was unable to monitor and control contractor performance.

## Why You Need a Functionally Integrated Team

I am going to add another requirement besides size to the owner team; the team has to be functionally integrated. *Functionally integrated* is a complicated term for a simple concept. There are two conditions required to be functionally integrated. First, all the skills needed to complete a project are present on the project team at the right time. Second, the team members have the ability and authority to perform their roles without having to check in with their boss every time they make a decision Think of a project team as the equivalent of a sports team playing a game. My favorite sport is baseball, which has nine players on the field at one time. The members of the baseball team work together to win the game, but each player has a specific job to do. The team has, for example, a pitcher, a catcher, and a shortstop; each of these positions requires specialized skills. A project without a functionally integrated team is the same as a baseball team playing the game without a shortstop or—more likely—a team with someone playing shortstop who is not very good at it. As you might suspect, projects done by functionally integrated teams have much better results than teams missing key players or players that cannot do their job.

Here is a perfect example of what happens when a team is not functionally integrated. In this example, the project team did not include a person from the maintenance organization responsible for keeping the facility operating smoothly. Having a maintenance person on board may not have seemed like a big deal at the time, but it ended up torpedoing the project. When the engineers designed the facility, they only left enough space for one to two people to work on the equipment at a time when the facility was shut down for routine maintenance. Leaving space for 6 to 10 people to work at a time could have saved the company $10 million in lost production for each shutdown by decreasing the time needed for maintenance work. From an engineering perspective, the goal is to only leave enough space between equipment to ensure the facility can be operated safely. Putting equipment closer together saved money by reducing the amount of land needed and the length of piping and other materials running between the equipment. The engineers did what they were trained to do, but there was no one there to tell them that the design would create a headache the business will have to live with for the life of the facility. The person who reviewed the engineer's design was the representative from the group that operates the facility. The operations group is responsible for running the facility, not maintaining it. When the operations representative reviewed and signed off on the design, he was only checking it from his own group's perspective. Essentially, he was filling in for the maintenance representative, but was not trained to do that job.

Projects led by functionally integrated project teams are just better than those led by nonintegrated teams. All things being equal, projects with functionally integrated teams build assets that have 10 percent better technical performance, are completed 15 percent faster, and are 10 percent cheaper. Everyone wants a project that is better, faster, and cheaper. A functionally integrated team is a practice that actually works to realize that goal.

## Help the Project Manager Get the Resources for a Functionally Integrated Team

An absolutely critical job for executives is getting the resources the project manager needs to build an integrated team. The hardest to fill owner team positions are those that are not under the direct control of the project management organization. Usually your project management group is responsible for staffing the core project team positions. These may include the project manager, the technical manager, project control lead, quality assurance/quality control lead, and disciplinary technical leads. But, depending on the project, your project may also need staff from sales and marketing, purchasing, finance, economics, or legal, for instance. For example, your project may need a lawyer full-time for six months because there are tricky intellectual property negotiations with some of the suppliers. Without your help, it may be difficult for the project manager to get the head of the legal department to assign someone to the project. The legal department has its own work to do, and unless extra staff members are available, the head of legal will probably be reluctant to assign someone to your project. The project manager most likely does not have the influence to get the resource. You may have to negotiate with or cajole the head of the legal department to get what you need. Together with the head of the legal department, you may have to develop a strategy to get the resource. Perhaps the company can hire someone temporarily to fill in for the person who will be assigned to your team.

The project manager has to be clear about all the people she needs, but your job is to work with the project manager and use your influence to get the best resources you can for the project.

## Do Not Outsource the Owner Team Role

It is tempting to outsource a large portion of the owner team to a contractor who will act on behalf of the owner to monitor progress, perform contract management services, and administer the change management process. The owner team maintains a smaller staff to make decisions and to take corrective action when progress deviates from the plan or changes occur. On the surface, this is an attractive strategy because it allows you to put a few of your people in leadership roles while using a contractor to do most of the work. Unfortunately, outsourcing the owner team tends to produce poor results because contractors, no matter how good they are, cannot be as effective as your own people at overseeing the project in its entirety. They will not scrutinize the actions of suppliers like your people would. They will not push back on contractor change orders as hard as your own people would. Also, when a contractor discovers a problem, even if they are as diligent as an owner in overseeing project activities, it will be harder for them to sound the alarm. They cannot garner the same level of attention within the owner organization to take corrective action. They will have to go through layers of their management to

| Intermediate Product (IP) Project | | Finished Product (FP) Project | |
| --- | --- | --- | --- |
| Project Director | 20 Months Late | Project Director | On Time |
| Project Team: Outsourced to a Contractor | 18% over Budget | Project Team: Owner Personnel Supplemented with Individuals outside the Company | On Budget |
| | Difficult Startup | | No Quality Problems |

**Figure 6.2 Outsourcing the Owner Team Led to Project Failure**

communicate a problem. Your own person would be able to go directly to the project manager and say there is a problem.

One of IPA's clients inadvertently ran an experiment that illustrates the danger of outsourcing the owner project team. The company had two big projects to do at the same time with limited staff. Although the projects were related, they were done by separate project directors. The first project was the Intermediate Product (IP) Project, which was building a chemical plant to make a product that would be used by the second project. The Finished Product (FP) Project would use the intermediate product along with other feedstocks to make a finished product. One project director chose to outsource the project team to a contractor; the other carefully built an owner team with the people who were available and hired individuals from outside the company to supplement the team.

The IP Project, with the outsourced owner team, was 20 months late, 18 percent over budget, and had difficulty starting up. At one point, the outsourced owner team reported that construction was 100 percent complete a full 12 months before construction was actually over (see Figure 6.2). The team clearly had no idea what the suppliers were doing and was not able to monitor and control their work.

In contrast, the FP Project was done on time and on budget and had no quality problems. The poor performance of the IP Project was not entirely the fault of the contractor, but they certainly had a large contribution to the failure. The result shows some of the risks of outsourcing your team. Things can get away from you fast because you do not have your people in place to spot problems. Tread carefully when developing strategies that put owner responsibilities into the hands of third parties.

## More Experienced Project Teams Do Better Projects

Besides the number of personnel, the experience of the owner team is also important. The notion that project teams staffed with more experienced people do higher-quality work is intuitive. Here are some data to support that intuition. I touched on the concept of project definition in Chapter 2, and I will go into much more detail in Chapter 7. As defined earlier, project definition is the process of converting the business requirements into a preliminary asset design and plans for doing the project. It gets the project team ready to execute so that project will be delivered within budget and on time. All things being equal, project teams with more experience take less time to complete project definition and produce a higher-quality result.[2] I am not suggesting that all experienced teams are successful or that all less experienced teams will fail, but experienced project teams usually better understand what work is required and how to get the work done.

## Strategies for Coping with Staffing Shortages

Of course, you will not always have the luxury of having as much experience as you would like. One strategy IPA has identified as being

[2]Lucas Milrod and Olivia Carr, "Doing More with Less (without Failing Miserably)" (annual meeting of the Upstream Industry Benchmarking Conference, IPA, November 2014).

successful is to leverage your experienced people with less experienced personnel in closely associated jobs. For example, on most projects, the project manager and design/engineering manager work closely together. The design manager in many respects is nearly the deputy project manager because so much of the total project, especially in the Define stage, involves design activities. A study done by IPA on team staffing shows that you can achieve good results by combining an experienced project manager with a less experienced design manager. Doing the opposite also works. You can put together a less experienced project manager with an experienced design manager. In either case, the experienced person is able to mentor the less experienced person. What clearly does not work is staffing both positions with inexperienced personnel. The staffing strategy has to account for the relative levels of experience in key leadership positions as it is developed.

Hiring experienced people for a project under contract to supplement your project team is also a viable, if less desirable, option for adding staff to a project team. These people are often close to retirement but not quite ready to stop working; they may have one or two more projects in them before they hit the golf course permanently. Finding the right person will require a careful search by your human resources department to match the person's skill set to the specifics of your project.

Using *hired guns* is an expensive option, especially during periods when capital activity is high, but you may have no choice if you want to do the project. The salaries of experienced project professionals may be outside the established salary ranges for comparable positions within your company. You may have to make the case to more senior management to get permission to pay these people more than what others make in the company. The contract the project professional signs has to include penalties for leaving before the project is complete (or incentives for staying until the project is complete). Also, the project sponsor's involvement in a project using a project manager under contract must be much higher to ensure that the project manager is making decisions that are aligned with the business goals for the project.

## Executives Working Together to Support the Project

So far I have discussed how executives (primarily the project sponsor) should support the project team. I am going to wrap up this chapter by describing what can be accomplished by executives working together to support a project team. I am going to share how a project achieved a spectacular result because of the level of cooperation between executives. The project was able to cut the capital cost by over 40 percent from what had been achieved previously, keeping the business competitive and able to maintain market share. Do not get me wrong. The project team performed admirably, but the team would have never found the solutions to cut costs so much without the leadership and teamwork of the executives.

When the business built its first manufacturing facility in Mainland China five years earlier, it had a total cost advantage from better manufacturing technology. However, over those five years, local competition eroded the cost advantage by building cheaper and cheaper facilities. To get started, the business chartered a functionally integrated project team to examine ways to significantly reduce capital costs without compromising health and safety or operating reliability.

The primary functions involved in the project, other than business, were operations, technology, project management, and procurement. Each of the leaders challenged their people to reexamine the assumptions that guided their work in the past. The leaders asked why it was done this way and whether it could be done differently to save money. In the end, the team found four areas ripe for cost reduction: (1) making the facility physically smaller, (2) using local standards,

(3) buying more equipment from local suppliers, and (4) forming a long-term partnership with an engineering contractor.

Executive involvement did not end there. The leaders had to continue to work together because none of these solutions could be implemented without getting agreement from other functions. Take, for example, the strategy for purchasing locally. Historically, the business had purchased key pieces of equipment from global manufacturers. Going with local suppliers meant working with less experienced companies with no proven track record. Project management was very concerned about the cost and schedule risk if the suppliers were unable to deliver equipment on time at the right quality. Technology had a concern about exposing the business's intellectual property to new suppliers. Operations was worried about the long-term reliability of the equipment. These were all legitimate concerns and would require management approval to implement the change. For this project, the executives formed a steering committee to review the project team's work and mediate any conflicts that arose when one group felt the strategy for reducing cost was too risky. Meeting as a group was an efficient way of clearing up each issue and getting in alignment. In the end, not only did the project cut costs, but it also was completed within budget, on schedule, and started up without incident.

Not every project can achieve results like this, and not every project needs as much executive support, but this example demonstrates that executives can play a major role in project success. It also strikes at the adage often expressed about how executives get teams to achieve astounding results. The adage goes like this—*Hire good people, give them clear goals, and get out of their way.* The implication is that executive meddling can only get in the way of a successful team. This is not entirely true for capital projects. Project teams need good people and clear goals, but they also need help to succeed.

# 7 Project Definition

The Fundamental Capital Project Concept Every Executive Must Understand

The quality of project definition at authorization is the best indicator of whether a project will come in on time, on budget, and meet specifications. A project with strong definition has done the work to identify the scope of work, has planned how the work will get done, and is prepared to start the execution stage. Achieving strong definition does not guarantee success; many things can still go wrong, especially if you or the project team become complacent, but the chances of success are much higher than for projects with weak project definition. Think of it this way: Strong project definition is the best insurance you have against the dreaded task of having to go to your boss or the board of directors to ask for more money or having to explain why the project is going to be very late. In this chapter, I will show how executives control the level of project definition reached at authorization. When you do not let—no, demand—that the project team complete the definition of the project before authorization, you are setting them and your project up to fail.

The basic concept of project definition is not hard to understand. Anyone who has tackled a home improvement project already understands it. Say you wanted to convert a bedroom into a home gym. One of your kids has graduated from college, and you have convinced yourself they will only be returning for the occasional visit. Project definition is deciding what equipment you want to include and figuring out what needs to be done to the room to make all the equipment fit and function. You do this work before you start buying the equipment and supplies so that you can estimate the cost before you make the final decision to go ahead with the project. You might have to cut back the scope if the cost is more than you want to spend.

The number of times you had to go back and forth to the store to get everything you needed is a good measure of how well you defined your project. Some people do an excellent job on project definition. They do not start until every detail is decided and the costs are meticulously added up. They only have to go to the store once. The equipment they bought for the gym all fits nicely, and they did not have to go back for more paint or anything else. They are happy with the result when the project is finished. The gym will definitely serve its purpose (provided they keep up the discipline to actually use it).

On the other side of the spectrum are people who go to the store and start buying stuff as soon as they get the idea. It may take them 10 trips back and forth before they get everything they need. When the project is finished, they probably have enough leftover material to convert another room to a gym, and, although all the equipment fits into the gym, the layout is not perfect. For example, getting on the treadmill means they have to make an awkward step over the weight bench.

Doing project definition for a sizable capital project is obviously more complex than a small home improvement project. As I defined in Chapter 2, project definition is the process of converting the business objectives into a project scope and strategy to design, build, and install the asset created or modified by the project to achieve the objectives. This work takes time and money to do it right. Take, for example, a $1 million project that is installing some new equipment. A project team will take about five months from the end of the Assess stage and spend between $30,000 and $50,000 (3 to 5 percent of the total project budget) to do all the project definition work necessary to get the project ready for execution. The execution stage of the project— from the time the project definition is complete until the asset is installed—will take about nine months.

Project definition transforms the work completed within the project frame into the scope of work and the project plans required to achieve your objectives for the project. If the project's primary objective is to modernize a business's inventory system, project definition identifies all the work that must be done to end up with an upgraded system, including how the tasks will be performed, by whom, and in what sequence. The project definition work is completed with enough detail to develop a final capital cost estimate within a certain plus or minus range that executives can use to evaluate the project's merits before making the final funding decision.

Project definition also gets a project team ready to move into the execution stage. This is a critical point. We take five months and spend $50,000 in project definition before doing the remainder of the project in nine months when we are going to spend the remaining $950,000. Just based on some rough calculations, we go from spending about $10,000 a month in project definition to more than $100,000 a month in project execution. That is a 10-fold increase in activity that happens very quickly. The project team staffs up and work begins on many activities in parallel. The project enters into binding contractual commitments to hire suppliers and purchase materials. The technical design is finalized. Preparation for construction, assembly, and installation begins. The group responsible for operating the asset when it is put into service starts its work to get ready.

A project team can be swamped with problems if they are not ready for the start of execution. Gaps in project definition can affect project execution in any number of ways. You might suffer from cost growth, schedule slip, asset performance shortfalls, or any combination of the above, but you never really know until it happens. I once reviewed a project that experienced approximately 25 percent cost growth because of construction rework. The root cause of the problem was a gap in project definition. The project team did not do a thorough job of assessing the technology supplier's capability. As soon as execution began, the technology supplier started to fall behind schedule. The team had to focus its attention on getting the technology supplier back on track. However, because it was distracted, the team was not able to monitor the work of another contractor doing engineering design in an unrelated area. The project team did not discover that contractor's errors until they started showing up in construction. All the work building foundations and structures had to be ripped out and redone because of the mistakes.

## Strong Project Definition Preserves Value and Produces Better Assets

The best way to understand the effect project definition has on a project is to contrast the performance of projects that were authorized with strong project definition with those with weak definition.[1] Recall from the first chapter that the average project loses about 12 percent of its value from cost and schedule overruns and asset performance problems. Projects with strong definition do not have any average losses cost, schedule, or asset performance issues, while projects with weak definition erode 25 percent of what was expected in those areas.

Perhaps even more important is the frequency of projects that lose 50 percent of their value because of project performance problems. One in 10 projects in IPA's database that I characterize as having strong definition lost 50 percent or more value, while one in four projects with weak definition suffered the same fate. This is a huge difference in the odds of having a disaster project. To lose 50 percent value means there is major cost growth, schedule slip, and asset performance problems. Projects in IPA's database that lost 50 percent of value after authorization just from project problems had an average budget overrun of 34 percent, an average schedule slip of 49 percent, and the asset was only able to operate at 72 percent when put into service. These were terrible projects by any measure. (See Figure 7.1.)

---

[1]Projects with strong project definition identified the complete scope of work and developed definitive project strategies. Projects with weak definition did not finish scope identification, did not complete project planning, or both.

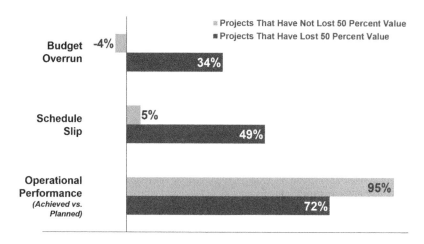

**Figure 7.1 Losing 50 Percent of Value Means Cost Overruns, Schedule Slip, and Asset Performance Problems**

## Build Better Performing Assets with Strong Project Definition

The real damage to a business when a project performs poorly can be the quality of the asset rather than cost and schedule overruns. Assets that are unable to run at full capacity, cannot meet product specifications, need more people than expected to run them, or require more maintenance have higher variable production costs than planned. Higher variable production costs are gifts that keep on giving. Over the life of the asset, unless more capital is invested to fix the problem, the profitability of every unit produced is lower than expected because of higher variable production costs.

The figure contains asset performance data specific to industrial facilities. It shows that projects with weak project definition were more expensive to run and maintain. These are facilities that do everything from processing oil and gas or precious metals, to producing chemicals, to manufacturing things like pharmaceuticals, toothpaste, and cookies. For industrial companies, the importance of variable production costs to the profitability of an investment is usually only second to product demand and product price. These data were collected one to three

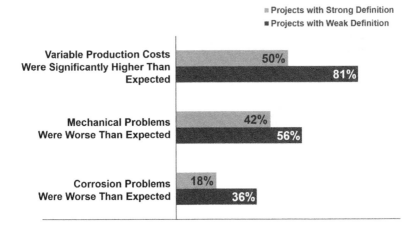

**Figure 7.2 Projects with Weak Definition Have Worse Than Expected Variable Production Costs and Maintenance Problems**

years after the asset was put into service. The results are the frequency of occurrence for each group. For example, corrosion problems were twice more likely for projects that had weak definition. (See Figure 7.2.)

Assets have higher than expected costs or problems for many reasons. After one project, the plant had to be run seven days a week instead of five days as planned to meet production targets because the product quality was not high enough when the plant was run at full rate. The consequence of slowing the plant down was higher energy use and higher operating personnel costs. In another example, maintenance costs were higher than expected because the very expensive filters in the process had to be replaced twice a year instead of once a year.

The relationship between asset performance and project definition is not limited to industrial projects. We surveyed users after IT projects were complete to get their assessment of the quality of the asset created by the project and found a strong correlation between project definition and the level of customer satisfaction when the project is complete.

The data show that you must factor in the risk of building an asset that never works quite right into your decisions. In my experience, this risk tends to fly under the radar of most executives. Considerable attention is paid to cost and schedule overruns, in part because they are immediately visible. Asset performance gaps, however, may not even be fully understood until after the project has been completed. For example, you may not know that your new office building's heat and air-conditioning system does not work correctly until the hottest days of summer or coldest days of winter. The economic analysis of a project being authorized with weak project definition has to consider the risk of asset performance problems to get a truer picture of the expected value.

## Executives Control the Quality of Project Definition

Executives determine the quality of project definition a project achieves in three basic ways:[2]

1. Clarity and consistency of objectives
2. The amount of money that is spent doing project definition
3. The amount of time that is spent doing project definition

Objectives are the instructions to the project team that describe what you want for the project. A project team cannot achieve strong project definition if you give them new instructions that affect scope and strategy. Changing objectives late in the game is like changing your improvement project from a home gym to a home office on the way to the store. Much of the work you did defining the gym project is

---

[2]This statement is predicated on having a competent project manager. A project manager must have enough knowledge of what strong project definition means, the work that needs to be done, in what sequence, and the resources required. The project manager then must have the skills to organize a team and make the work happen. Get yourself a new project manager if this is not the case.

no longer useful and has to be done again. Most actual projects do not change objectives as drastically as that, but even subtle changes to objectives can undo a significant amount of project definition work. This is because projects are a complicated series of interrelated activities and events; any change can make the whole system go out of kilter. I evaluated one software project that started with an objective to deliver services through a desktop application. However, as the project proceeded, customer feedback was that they much preferred a web-based solution. The project lost a year to redo all the project definition work to develop a web-based tool.

## Understand the Cost of Weak Project Definition

Doing a thorough job on project definition usually means spending 3 to 5 percent of the total capital cost before the project is funded. The cost is mainly for the project team and the third-party service suppliers needed to get the work done.

Understandably, executives are cautious about making this up-front investment for project definition when there is a real chance the project may never get funded. Say you are waiting for the results of ongoing consumer product testing; negative feedback will scuttle the project. Canceling the project means all the money spent on project definition has to be written off as an expense.

Often executives view the money spent on project definition as being wasted if the project is canceled. This really is not true. In my example, there would have been no chance of delivering the new product when needed if the consumer product testing had been positive. Starting project definition after the results were in would delay the completion of the project. In this case, deciding to complete project definition while waiting for the results is very much like buying an option to purchase a financial instrument or some commodity. An option is a contract that gives you the right but not the obligation to purchase the underlying asset at a specific price by a certain date. If the price of the asset increases over the price specified in the option, you exercise the option. If not, you let the option expire and you lose the money spent to buy the option. Not all options end up as assets you own, but that does not mean you won't ever buy options. It's the same way for project definition.

Another way to look at the issue is from a portfolio perspective. Although the risk of sunk costs from a late cancellation of an individual project exists, strong project definition pays for itself many times over in a project portfolio. Let's say a project with weak definition costs a total of $1 million. Based on IPA's historical data, that exact same project with strong definition, on average, will cost 8 percent less, or approximately $920,000, including the money spent on project definition. The project is cheaper because the team is able to develop more efficient strategies and avoid rework to fix problems. Even if a business spent 5 percent of the total cost to define two independent $1 million projects, they would still be $30,000 better off even if one of the projects was canceled. (See Table 7.1.)

You still do not want to economize on project definition costs even if you do not care about the cost savings. Here is one example in which the strategy to minimize project definition costs produced a major disaster for the business. For this project, the economic feasibility of the project rested on price negotiations with a dedicated customer for the product. Without a high enough price, the gross profit would not cover the project's capital cost. Because commercial negotiations were ongoing, the business unit was only willing to spend a little money to define the scope and project strategy. The team had a budget

**Table 7.1  Strong Project Definition Pays Off Quickly**

| | |
|---|---|
| Savings from first project with strong definition | $80,000 |
| Wasted cost from canceled second project | −$50,000 |
| Total savings | $30,000 |

of 1 percent of the total installed cost for project definition (as I said, a typical project spends between 3 to 5 percent of the total installed cost to do project definition). Without the funds to do much work, the project team cobbled together a high-level engineering design and plans for how the project would be done. As it turned out, price negotiations were successful, and the project was authorized for execution. The project ran into problems as soon as it moved into the next stage. The team discovered that additional scope was needed, materials and labor were grossly underestimated, the contractors selected by the team were unable to perform the work as planned, and a delayed construction permit added three months to the project schedule. The project required three supplemental funding requests to be completed, eventually exceeding its budget by 85 percent with an eight-month schedule delay. The company turned to IPA after this debacle to help them with their corporate strategy for project definition.

## Be Careful When Trading Fast Schedule for Strong Project Definition

Besides money, you need time to complete project definition. It takes time to do the economic and technical studies to choose between alternatives, it takes time to develop preliminary designs and to plan project strategy, and, finally, it takes time to prepare the capital cost estimate executives use to make the final investment decision.

Unfortunately, time can be a more precious commodity than the money when there is schedule pressure to get the project done by a certain date. For example, companies that make agricultural fertilizers and pesticides that do not have their inventories full in time for the spring planting season will miss their revenue opportunity. Food manufacturers that make cookies and other desserts sell as much as 40 to 50 percent of their yearly sales during the holiday season. They

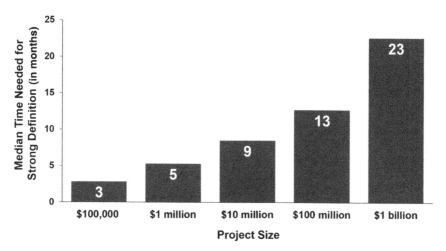

**Figure 7.3 Time Needed for Strong Project Definition Depends on Project Size**

need their factories up and running by a certain date or they will not get shelf space in the supermarket. If these companies do not hit their seasonal window, the project is not worth doing. There can be schedule pressure when a competitor announces they are rolling out a new technology or introducing a new product. The business risks a sustained loss of market share if they do not react in time to head off the competitor's action.

Often the only way to significantly shorten a project schedule is to cut the time spent defining the project before starting execution. For some perspective, I am showing the median duration for projects in IPA's databases to reach a strong level of project definition.[3] (See Figure 7.3.)

---

[3]These are just averages from projects in IPA's database. Any individual project may need more or less time, depending on the nature and complexity of the project. For example, a $1 million project that includes new technology or must go through a series of public hearings to receive permits may take much longer than five months.

Reducing the time spent in project definition often means making compromises about the quality of the project definition work. Let's say you have a $10 million project, which typically takes nine months to finish project definition. You could attempt to shorten the schedule by doing the work in five months instead of nine months. Adding extra people to the project team will get the work done faster, but to really save time, you will be forced to skip some work or do things out of order. For example, a key project definition task is to gather technical information about the site where the asset will be built. If your project is constructing a new building, the engineers need to know the condition of the land before they start designing the building. They need information on the level of the water table, the type of soil present, and whether there are any abnormalities, perhaps large rocks, just underneath the surface. This information is collected by doing tests at the site before engineers start designing the building foundation. To save time, the project team could skip the tests and design the foundations based on a set of assumptions about the location. Perhaps they assume there are no large rocks that have to be blasted away or that the soil is clay instead of sand. If they are right, you managed to save time without facing any consequences. If they are wrong, you may have to redesign the foundation and do a lot more work to get the site ready for the building. Project definition has a "natural sequence" that cannot be avoided without potential problems.

Projects with weak definition typically erode 25 percent of the economic value because costs are higher, schedules are longer, or asset performance is worse than expected even when we think we are accounting for the risk. For one in four projects, the risks are much, much higher than expected. The risks capital projects face are often just too complex for us to foresee all the consequences of the compromises made to shorten project definition. Spend enough time around projects and you will be amazed at how frequently there are boulders—literally or figuratively—just under the surface that you did not see, but could have with strong project definition.

Taking risk is an integral part of creating value for shareholders, and I am not suggesting that businesses should always avoid the risk of trading faster schedule for weaker project definition. However, you can make better decisions about the trade-offs you make by working more closely with your project team. The first thing you should do is have the project team identify the areas that are most vulnerable to weak project definition. They should walk you through what could happen if some of the key assumptions turn out to be wrong. Remember, however, that people tend to underestimate the probability and consequences of future bad events. Project managers and other project leaders are no different. You can force a more realistic discussion of how bad something could get by using lessons learned from similar situations, by including someone outside the team to play the devil's advocate, or by asking your team for factual benchmarking statistics.

Another strategy is to choose to make a different trade-off rather than fast schedule versus project risk. For example, one way to shorten project definition is to make the project easier. Say you are buying new accounting software because your current system is obsolete and could fail at any time, leaving you without the ability to manage the company. Of course, while you are installing a new system, you probably also want to make a number of upgrades at the same time, but the upgrades will lengthen project definition considerably as you design the new system. To save time in project definition, you could purchase an off-the-shelf system that meets most of your needs rather than giving you everything you want. The new accounting system will not be as efficient as it could be, but you will have avoided a major disruption to your operation.

## Reduce the Number of Schedule-Driven Projects

One way to ensure that project definition is not routinely compromised is to reduce the number of schedule-driven projects in your company's portfolio. Businesses may do more schedule-driven projects than necessary just because there is a problem somewhere in the system. Executives may make promises to shareholders or customers that create hopelessly optimistic schedule targets, dooming the project to failure before it even starts. A culprit for many IPA clients is that their business planning process does not identify and turn over opportunities early enough to provide their teams sufficient time to complete project definition. For other companies, the project organization is not large enough or sufficiently skilled to complete the work efficiently, thereby increasing the time required for project definition. Problems with cross-organizational cooperation can also slow things down. For one of my clients, the operations group was routinely adding two months to project definition because they were not providing timely input to the project teams. To minimize the number of schedule-driven projects, executives need to carefully monitor the reasons and take corrective action as necessary.

For the projects that are truly schedule driven, the business and the project organization can work closely together to deliver what the business needs. One other benefit of reducing the number of schedule-driven projects is that it frees up the best resources for the projects that need them rather than spreading them out over many projects.

## More Project Definition Is Not Necessarily Better

I am going to close this chapter with a caution that you can do too much project definition before a project is authorized. Think of the story of Goldilocks and the Three Bears. But instead of the porridge being too hot, too cold, or just right, a project can do too little, too much, or just the right amount of project definition. For almost all projects, strong definition is just the right amount. It represents the best trade-off between risking the up-front investment to define the project and the benefit of risk reduction. Spending more money and time to achieve a level of definition beyond strong usually does not get you much benefit.

You would only get value under two conditions. The first condition is that the extra time and money makes a meaningful improvement in the accuracy of the investment analysis used to make the authorization decision. The second condition is that the executives making the investment decision care about the reduction of uncertainty. An example should help. Let's say a project is ready for authorization, the project has strong definition, and the risk analysis of the cost estimate indicates the estimate accuracy is plus 15 percent, minus 10 percent. I will go into much more detail in the chapter on cost estimating about what this range means, but, for now, let's just say that a business expects that a project authorized for $10 million with a plus 15 percent, minus 10 percent range will finish between $11.5 million and $9 million most of the time. Although executives would be happier if the project finished closer to $9 million than $11.5 million, the business case is still robust at the higher cost.

Spending the time and money to improve project definition to increase the accuracy of the cost estimate is very unlikely to change the decision to authorize the project. Although there is a small chance that the project team will find some scope or risks that it missed by doing the additional definition that would push the updated cost estimate above $11.5 million, it is unlikely. Say the next cost estimate is $10.25 million, plus 10 percent, minus 5 percent. The executives would still make the same investment decision.

All that has been accomplished is adding to the sunk costs if the project is canceled for other reasons. It may have cost another 5 percent of the total budget and 3 months to get the cost estimate to a plus 10 percent, minus 5 percent range. That is on top of the 5 percent spent to get to a strong level of definition. As long as the project is not canceled, that additional money is not really wasted. The primary way the cost estimate accuracy is improved after reaching strong definition is by doing the tasks usually reserved for the start of project execution, mainly doing more of the technical design. That work is still used if the project is approved. But what happens if there is market downturn or a client backs out of a contract just as the project is ready for authorization? Instead of throwing away 5 percent of the total cost, 10 percent now has to be written off.

One of the benefits of having a portfolio of capital projects is that the value eroded on some projects because of cost overruns is balanced by underruns on other projects. The overall portfolio will deliver the value expected and the overall capital budget will be on target. This allows executives to be more neutral when considering individual project risk. Unless a project represents such a large investment that negative results are material to the overall health of the company, there should be no reason to achieve better than a strong level of definition by authorization. Remember, however, portfolio results are only normally distributed when projects routinely reach a strong level of definition at authorization. Authorizing too many projects with weak definition will mean the average project will erode value, causing a negative skew in the portfolio's performance.

Executives without a portfolio of projects need to decide what level of accuracy in the investment analysis they want to achieve by authorization so the plans can be laid out to achieve that target. Spending more time and money for additional definition before committing to the project may be justified for the capital projects where overruns of the cost and schedule or shortfalls in asset performance threaten the financial health of the company.

# 8 It's Going to Cost How Much!?!

A Guide to Help Executives Avoid Capital Cost Surprises

I use this joke sometimes when I talk about cost estimate accuracy in some of my presentations:

*Three cost estimators get some time off from work and decide to go duck hunting. The three estimators are sitting in a duck blind and a duck flies by. The first estimator shoots and misses 15 feet to the right. The second estimator shoots and misses 15 feet to the left. The third estimator yells, "We got 'em!"*

This joke gets a laugh every time I tell it to cost estimators. Executives, however, don't find it so funny. Their different responses tell you something about their different points of view. Cost estimators view a cost estimate as a forecast that has an accuracy range determined through analysis. If the actual cost is within the estimate's stated range, cost estimators will consider that to be a success. Executives are more focused—understandably—on coming in on budget, meaning the final number is at or below the estimated cost.

Unfortunately, the cost estimator's point of view is more correct. Estimates are predictions, just like a prediction for tomorrow's high temperature. A single value prediction will almost certainly be wrong. For every 1,000 projects in IPA's database, one will come in exactly on budget, and, probably for that one project, some accountant just rounded the final number up or down!

A big mistake made by executives is not understanding the chance that the actual capital cost of a project will be higher, sometimes much higher, than they expect. You have to factor the accuracy of a cost estimate into your decisions. For example, say you have a cost estimate for $10 million and, given the estimate's accuracy, there is a 25 percent chance the final cost will be more than $11 million and a 10 percent chance the final cost will be as much as $12.5 million.

Are you okay with this? For your company, a $10 million project may be a small investment, and although the business case for this project will be hurt if costs are higher, the business can absorb the overrun.

Your attitude is probably different if $10 million is a major investment. Perhaps you will not be bothered too much if the cost grows to $11 million. The business case is solid, and you will still make money at the higher amount. But, if the costs are higher than $11 million, the economics will not look so good and you will have to find somewhere in the company budget to pay for the overrun. You might even have to delay or cancel another project or borrow the money to pay for it. If you cannot take a chance of spending more than $11 million, something has to be done to reduce that risk. There are many things you could do. For example, you could change the business objectives so that the scope can be reduced, thereby reducing the chances of spending more than $11 million. The one thing you should *not* do is to ignore the uncertainty and hope for the best.

## Key Concepts to Understand about Capital Cost Estimate Accuracy

I cannot make you an expert on cost estimates in one chapter, but I can help you to ask better questions so that you can use the information to make good decisions. This is a difficult subject, but it is worthwhile learning. Here are the concepts I am going to cover in the chapter:

- Factor the estimate range into project decision making
- Improve project definition to narrow the range
- Rules for getting contingency right

You need to understand these concepts so that you can correctly interpret and act on the information being provided to you by the project manager or cost estimator.

## Factor the Cost Estimate Range into Decision Making

A capital project cost estimate is really a distribution of possible outcomes, not a single value. We typically think of the cost estimate as a single number. For example, the project manager may tell you the cost estimate is $10 million, but unless the project is all but over, there is the potential that the final cost of that project will be higher or lower than $10 million. Estimate accuracy indicates how much the final cost may vary from the $10 million number. An illustration of the possible locations where a hurricane might make landfall is a good way to think about cost estimate ranges. The illustration shows the position of the hurricane on Monday evening and projects the path where the hurricane might reach landfall in the United States by Saturday morning, five days later. (See Figure 8.1.)

**Figure 8.1  Cone of Uncertainty for Hurricane Approaching the U.S. Gulf Coast**

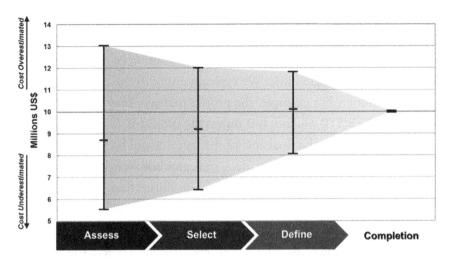

**Figure 8.2   Cost Estimate Accuracy Improves at Each Stage-Gate**

The possible path of the hurricane is referred to as the *cone of uncertainty*. The cone of uncertainty for possible landfall on the U.S. Gulf Coast stretches roughly 500 miles, all the way from Corpus Christi, Texas, to New Orleans, Louisiana, a very wide range. You will notice that the cone of uncertainty is much narrower for Tuesday evening, only one day later, and gets progressively wider until Saturday morning.

Cost estimates have a cone of uncertainty very similar to that of hurricanes. Figure 8.2 shows the cone of uncertainty for capital cost estimates for projects in IPA's database.[1] The ranges shown in the chart are based on a project that had an *actual* cost of $10 million.

The ranges shown in the figure represent the typical accuracy of the cost estimates prepared at each stage-gate. Here is how to interpret the chart. At the Assess gate, about 10 percent of the time, the cost for

---

[1] Figure 8.2 is based on IPA data for 102 completed projects for which IPA had the cost estimate (the base estimate plus contingency) at each of the major stage-gates. The points in the range are the p10 and p90 points of the cost estimate distribution for the 102 cost estimates.

a project that eventually finished at $10 million will be estimated at $13 million, or $3 million too high. That means the project cost dropped about 23 percent, $13 million to $10 million, over the life of the project to when it was completed. At the other end of the range, the initial cost estimate will be $5.6 million for a project that finishes at $10 million, meaning the cost estimate grew about 80 percent over the life of the project. Another way of expressing the estimate range at the Assess gate based on this data would be to say the range is minus 23 percent, plus 80 percent.

As you can see, the range is not normally distributed at every stage-gate. Project cost is underestimated much more frequently than overestimated. The skew, especially at the Assess gate, is expected. Often, at that point, there is only a hazy understanding of the project scope. Getting centered is very difficult unless you are working with good analogues. There are many more ways to be too low in the cost estimate than to be too high. At the Select and Define gates, however, the skew is often caused by poor estimating and contingency setting methods. I will go into this topic in more detail later in the chapter.

## The Cone of Uncertainty Progressively Narrows

The cone narrows substantially from the Assess gate to the Define gate as more detail is added to the project's definition. For example, the estimates range from $5.6 million to $13 million at the Assess gate. By the time we get to the Define gate, the estimate is between $8.1 million and $11.8 million, a substantial improvement. One driver of the reduction in the range is the level of technical design completed at each stage. For example, a project at the Assess gate usually has 1 or 2 percent of the technical design complete. At the end of Define, it is more likely to be 15 to 25 percent. As you can see, the additional detail makes the cost estimates more precise.

This is one of the key features of the stage-gate process. As more detail is added to the technical design and other areas of project planning, the certainty of the cost estimate improves. It provides executives with more confidence that they are making the right decision as the level of financial commitment increases.

## Develop Your Own Cone of Uncertainty

Every business that routinely does capital projects should have its own cone of uncertainty based on the results of its own projects.[2] The data will show the accuracy of the cost estimates at each gate based on the strengths and weaknesses of your own project system. As I will discuss later, the use of empirical data, especially your own, is the best way to establish the contingency required for a cost estimate. You should be concerned if no one at your company can show how cost estimates progress through your system. It probably means your business's capability to develop and execute capital projects is not very good.

Not every project will follow the exact pattern I am showing here. The cone of uncertainty will be narrower at the Assess gate for certain types of projects. For example, a project that is replacing existing equipment and has a known scope of work probably has a more accurate cost estimate at the Assess gate than typical.

Businesses that have maintained cost estimating competency and cost estimating tools are also likely to produce more accurate cost estimates at each stage-gate. Businesses with more capital project capability and discipline will also tend to have more accurate cost estimates because the information used to develop the cost is higher

---

[2]Public sources of cost data can be used to generate a cone of uncertainty that is specific to your industry and type of project if you do not capture your own data or you do not do capital projects routinely. You do have to be careful with this data because it tends to be biased, but it can provide a starting point.

quality, and their project teams will be able to do a better job of identifying risks and preventing them from causing cost growth.

## Insist the Investment Analysis Include the Full Range of the Estimate

Here is a test for you. Open up a recent business case and look at the cost estimate range used in the investment analysis. The investment analysis that calculates the expected return on investment for a project usually includes a risk analysis to show how variations in the key financial variables affect the return on investment. For example, the risk analysis will show what would happen to the return on investment if product prices were 20 percent higher than the value used in the investment analysis.

In my experience, the range used for the cost estimate (and the schedule estimate for that matter) is almost always too narrow. Often I see plus or minus 10 percent as the range applied to the cost estimate. For example, if the cost estimate is $10 million, the risk analysis will show the effect on the return on investment if project costs grow to $11 million or fall to $9 million. Executives use the results of the risk analysis to decide whether the risk of a cost overrun is acceptable.

The data I have presented suggest that a plus or minus 10 percent range grossly understates the cost risk and the potential for a lower than expected return on investment. Table 8.1 translates the cone of uncertainty into estimate ranges at each stage-gate.

### Table 8.1 Cost Estimate Accuracy at Each Stage-Gate

|        | Plus | Minus |
|--------|------|-------|
| Assess | +80  | −23   |
| Select | +55  | −16   |
| Define | +23  | −15   |

The main takeaway here is that it is very rare to actually have an estimate that is plus or minus 10 percent. Even at the Define gate, the typical cost estimate has an accuracy range of minus 15 percent to plus 23 percent. Testing the project economics at only plus 10 percent instead of plus 20 percent means executives are not prepared for the chance of lower financial returns.

You have to ask questions to understand the cost estimate range as you make project decisions to fully understand the full potential for higher costs. The example that follows highlights the problem of not factoring the estimate range into project decision making.

## Be Careful Making Commitments Based on the Assess Gate Estimate

Executives often want to make a commitment to a project based on that initial estimate at the Assess gate. For example, a customer may want a signed contract from the business that they will supply the product by a certain date. Sometimes a capital project is just one part of a business venture. For example, launching a new product requires retooling of the business's entire supply chain and an extensive marketing campaign. These other activities have to start at the same time, making it hard to wait for a better cost estimate. Often, the business just wants to know whether this project will help it meet its performance targets. If not, the business will move on to something else. The problem is that the range at the Assess gate is so wide you can find yourself committed to a project that ends up costing much more than you expected, even if you have a strong cost estimating system. The next short example is representative of what happens many times on capital projects. The business effectively commits to a project based on the Assess stage-gate cost estimate without developing any plans for the possibility the cost will grow later.

The business had developed a new, healthier product in its line of frozen meals. Market analysis and consumer testing indicated that demand for the product was strong, so a project to build a brand-new flexible production line was quickly initiated. The project's number one priority was getting production online as soon as possible to meet the anticipated demand. The Assess estimate—based on high-level engineering and planning work—was approximately $45 million. At $45 million, the business was willing to do the project. They commissioned a project team to start designing the flexible production line and ordered equipment that would take a long time to deliver to accelerate the schedule. Over the next two months, as the project team progressed the design, the cost estimate grew to $60 million as the full cost for the production flexibility, schedule acceleration, and additional scope items missed in the earlier estimate were added in. The growth in the cost estimate should not have been a huge surprise. As mentioned earlier, it's much more likely that estimates will be too low when the full scope of work is not known.

The project manager told IPA that the project sponsor literally choked when the project team presented the new estimate. Soon after, the team was directed by the business to find a more affordable option. The change meant paying a $2 million cancellation fee to the equipment vendor. The business was not happy about paying the fee but had no choice. The change in scope meant the equipment was no longer needed. The project team estimated about $1 million was spent developing a design that was tossed away.

With some rework, the project team got the cost down to $50 million, something the business could afford. The eventual solution was to convert some existing equipment to the new service rather than building an all-new line. The project was eventually completed with good results about six months later than the original plan.

In this particular example, the business never even considered the possibility that the capital cost would increase after the initial estimate and that they would have to pay the cancellation fee on the equipment.

The other major mistake they made was not sharing the maximum budget with the project team. The upper limit of what they could afford, $50 million, was only 11 percent more than the initial estimate. Even a carefully prepared Assess stage-gate estimate would have a strong chance of increasing past $50 million. If they had shared the maximum budget, the project team would have started looking for a cheaper option on day one.

## Improve Project Definition to Narrow the Cost Estimate Range

The question you probably have is: *How do I narrow the cost estimate range and reduce the tendency to underestimate the cost?* The answer is to achieve a better level of project definition at each stage-gate. As I said in Chapter 2 when I was describing the stage-gate process, each stage-gate has a set of requirements for the type and amount of work that needs to be completed to pass the gate. The requirements are not arbitrary. They are established so that the cost estimate produced at the stage-gate has an acceptable range for the decision and financial commitment being made at that stage-gate.

In Chapter 7, I introduced the concept that the level of project definition can be either strong or weak. As the names suggest, projects with strong definition have met the requirements at each stage-gate, while projects with weak definition have not. Table 8.2 shows the

**Table 8.2  Strong Project Definition Improves Cost Estimate Accuracy**

|       | Select Gate Definition | | Define Gate Definition | |
|-------|------|--------|------|--------|
|       | Weak | Strong | Weak | Strong |
| Plus  | 77%  | 38%    | 29%  | 19%    |
| Minus | −17% | −15%   | −15% | −15%   |

estimate range for projects at the Select and Define gates for each category, strong and weak project definition.[3]

In each case, the estimate range is narrower with strong definition. In particular, the high side of the range is reduced because better project definition reduces the risks that cause the project cost to overrun. You probably notice that the low side of the range does not change much, depending on the level of project definition. This happens because cost estimates are bounded on the low side. You cannot spend less than zero on something, but you can spend infinitely more than what you expected.

There are two very important conclusions from the data I just showed. First, you will probably be out of luck if you are expecting costs to go down to make the business case economically viable. Unless you change the business objectives so that the scope of work is cut, the costs will probably not decline. Once we get past the Select gate, there are no painless ways of finding big savings.

Second, projects with weak definition are riskier, and the data show that the potential for a big overrun is much higher, especially at the Select gate, where the high side of the estimate range for weak definition is two times higher than for strong project definition. And, as I will show you in the next section, even when we know the risk exists, the method we use to lower the risk of an overrun (setting contingency) does not prevent the overrun from occurring. As an executive responsible for capital, you have to ask yourself the following questions: *Why are we allowing the project to move to the next stage if the requirements have not been met? What is gained by taking on this additional risk?* If there is a justification for the additional risk, you better make sure the contingency in the estimate reflects that risk. As I describe next, history suggests this rarely happens.

---

[3]I do not have enough completed projects with Assess gate cost estimates to relate the estimate range at this point to the level of project definition.

## Contingency Requirements Are Usually Underestimated When Project Definition Is Weak

Contingency is money added to a cost estimate to reduce risk of an overrun of the cost estimate and is money that you *expect* to be spent. Contingency does not reduce the estimate range or improve the estimate's accuracy. All it does is increase the single value we use to represent the project's cost estimate so that the chance of an overrun is reduced. For example, let's say a project with $1 million estimate has a 60 percent chance of an overrun. By adding, say, $50,000 to the estimate, we can reduce the chance of the final cost being more than $1 million to 50 percent. We could add even more money to reduce the chance of the overrun to a lower percentage: $100,000, say, brings the chance of an overrun to 30 percent.[4]

The amount of contingency a project needs increases with the level of project cost risk; yet, companies rarely increase contingency to reflect project risk. Take, for example, a project at the Select gate. For industrial projects, a project with a strong level of project definition at Select will need about 15 percent contingency to have a 50/50 chance of not overrunning the estimate. That same project with weak definition will need approximately 28 percent contingency because of the additional uncertainty in the cost estimate. That is a huge difference in contingency requirements. Guess how much contingency is actually added to the estimates in the weak and strong project definition categories? In both cases, it is 15 percent! (See Table 8.3.)

In other words, projects with totally different risk profiles typically get the same amount of contingency. The projects with strong definition get what they need to prevent an overrun on

---

[4]This paper does an excellent job of explaining contingency in more detail: Larry R. Dysert, "Is 'Estimate Accuracy' an Oxymoron?" (AACE International Transactions, 2006).

**Table 8.3 Overall Project Risk Is Usually Underestimated When Project Definition Is Weak**

| Select Gate Estimates | Weak Definition | Strong Definition |
|---|---|---|
| Average Contingency Added | 15% | 15% |
| Average Contingency Required | 28% | 15% |

average. Projects with weak definition get too little. How is this possible? How could the project risk be missed by such a wide margin?

The reason is a combination of two factors. The first, and most important, factor is the method most commonly used to evaluate contingency requirements: a Monte Carlo simulation applied to individual estimate line items or subtotals. This method is not effective when project definition is weak. The tool does not account for the systemic risk created by poor project definition.[5] In a nutshell, the tool is good at calculating how project-specific risks such as bad weather might increase the cost of construction, but it misses the effect of how poor project definition may make many things in the cost estimate more expensive.

Second, project sponsors, or the executives more senior to the project sponsor, sometimes exert pressure on project teams to minimize contingency to keep the cost within an acceptable budget. Even if there is no pressure, executives rarely push project teams to request *more* contingency than they are asking for even when they need it.

---

[5]This paper developed by IPA will explain in more detail: Scott E. Burroughs and Gob Juntima, "Exploring Techniques for Contingency Setting" (AACE International Transactions, 2004).

Establishing the amount of contingency in an estimate is one of the most difficult and contentious project activities. The analysis to support contingency setting is hard because it involves forecasting what events will occur and what impact they will have on the project if they do occur. The activity is contentious because, as you would expect, there will always be different views on all of the factors that influence how much contingency a project needs.

Debate about the amount of contingency needed is good if it creates awareness and alignment on how much contingency should be included. Too often, however, it degrades into a game in which different parties try to gain advantage. Next, I will explain how you can avoid or at least reduce these problems.

## Follow These Rules to Get Contingency Right

Besides improving the discipline for the level of project definition at the stage-gate, here are six ways (described in more detail next) to get the right amount of contingency:

- Insist that the risk analysis done to set contingency has some empirical basis.
- Set contingency to have the same chance of an overrun as it does of an underrun.
- Use robust project controls to establish undistorted control budgets and gain transparency on how contingency is being used.
- Recognize that contingency does not cover business-driven scope changes.
- Use management reserve rather than adding contingency beyond what is expected to be spent to reduce the chances of an overrun.
- Accept that overruns will happen; punish only for not knowing why costs are what they are.

## Insist That the Risk Analysis Has Some Empirical Basis

Ask the project manager and the cost estimator to supplement the contingency analysis by using your company's data or general industry data. You could ask them to answer the following questions:

- How much contingency do our projects or projects like ours typically need to prevent an overrun at this stage-gate? How does the level of contingency you are proposing compare?

- How do the level of project definition and other risk drivers for this project compare to those of our other projects? Is the definition worse, better, or the same as for our typical project?

- What is the cause when our projects overrun? Do we miss big cost risks in the estimate? Was the project team unable to respond to emerging risks?

Empirical data in the form of project cost histories can be used to calculate contingency requirements, or, if nothing else, they can be used to vet the contingency analysis produced by other methods.

## Set Contingency to Have the Same Chance of an Overrun as an Underrun

Executives have to navigate the process of setting contingency carefully. Including more contingency than a project needs allows project teams to relax and not focus enough on minimizing project cost. For instance, if the included contingency is high, the team may not negotiate as hard with suppliers to get the best price. It also creates a slush fund that gets used by stakeholders like operations or maintenance to upgrade the project scope or existing facilities. As a result, you will end up paying more money than necessary to get what you want. I worked on one project that built a warehouse for the maintenance group with the money left over in the budget. It may sound extreme, but this type of thing happens frequently.

On the other hand, executives who try to reduce contingency below what is reasonable just incentivize the project manager, project team, and cost estimators to hide the money in other parts of the estimate where it is hard to detect, which detracts from cost-control efforts.

## Use Robust Project Controls

So far in the book, I have highlighted three main practices that improve the chances of project success: (1) clear objectives, (2) an integrated project team, and (3) good project definition. Project control is a fourth practice. Project control includes the activities that track actual project performance against plan by collecting data, comparing to the plan, documenting the variance, and using the data to recommend corrective actions and develop forecasts of the likely outcomes. A major part of project control is tracking actual costs against estimated costs. A robust project control process starts with a realistic budget (a budget without gaming or distortion). It then makes transparent through change control how contingency is being used by providing a detailed accounting of the money. The project manager is responsible for project control, but if you are really worried that contingency will become a slush fund, you should read the basis of estimate report at the start and then the project control reports that are produced during execution. Ask questions if it is not clear where contingency is being used.

## Recognize That Contingency Does Not Pay for Business-Driven Scope Changes

Contingency accounts for risk that we know exists but cannot be pinned to a specific part of the estimate. For example, at the Select gate, 5 to 10 percent of the total technical design is typically complete. At that level of definition, the project team may underestimate the infrastructure needed to support the asset. In another project, the project team may undersize a major piece of equipment. History tells that we should expect these types of errors and omissions, but we do not know exactly what they are until they occur.

Contingency does not cover cost increases that result from changes to objectives. For example, say you are building a new office complex and you decide to add a laboratory to the project. It would be very difficult for the cost estimator to anticipate that you are going to make a change or what change you might make. You have to add the cost of the scope change to the cost estimate and keep the same level of contingency. You might even need to add more contingency if the change adds more cost risk.

## Use Management Reserve to Lower the Chances of an Overrun

You can use management reserve rather than adding contingency as a way of reducing the risk of an overrun while keeping contingency at a 50/50 level. Management reserve is money that is added to the project cost used in the project's investment analysis (and funded) but is not released to the project team until needed. Management reserve is for identified risks that may or may not materialize. Say there is a chance that the government will issue new environmental regulations just before the project is to receive its permit. Meeting the new requirements may mean adding scope or it may cause a significant disruption to the project schedule (or both). The extra money needed to meet the new requirements is only released to the team if these requirements actually change. Management reserve allows you to keep the money in your control until it is needed.

## Accept That Overruns Will Happen

A project system that has an equal number of overruns as underruns is actually a healthy sign. It means that the cost estimates that are prepared for authorization are unbiased; that is, they are good faith estimates of what the project should cost. Your project managers will never perform effective risk analysis and give a full, truthful accounting of the contingency they need if you insist that all projects underrun or only allow a small overrun of 5 or 10 percent before someone gets in trouble. If you really do this, the project system is so punitive that you will get no overruns, and you will end up spending more to build your assets. Project managers will bury contingency in the base estimate where it cannot be controlled, thereby reducing the discipline to minimize costs.

As I discussed, 1 in 10 projects overruns by 25 percent or more. Plan on it. I am not suggesting that project managers should not be accountable for the project budget. But you have to accept that overruns will occur and sometimes the reason for the overrun is outside the project manager's control. For example, every couple of years at least one project that IPA evaluates has a piece of major equipment that was manufactured overseas literally fall off the boat as it is being shipped to the project site. Imagine the problem that creates! The problem is not the cost of the equipment. That is usually covered by insurance. The problem is that now the entire project is delayed. The business gets its asset late, the project team is on the job longer, and suppliers ask for extra money because their own work is delayed. Luckily, this is a rare event, but every project has unexpected events that sometimes lead to much higher overall costs.

When a big overrun happens, you need to understand why it occurred; only hold the project manager accountable for poor performance and/or mismanagement of the risks as they presented themselves.

When you insist on underruns, you create a high conservative risk-averse project system. It is important to realize that most project managers feel enormous accountability for project outcomes—often more than they really can control or be justifiably held accountable for.

Keep in mind that we often give project managers a poor hand to play with. In fact, the most significant and perhaps most common risk is a weak project system (lack of skilled resources, inadequate systems and tools, and slow decision making), which can only be improved by executives.

# 9 Using a Project Steering Committee to Improve Executive Decision Making

The best way to leverage your time overseeing a capital project is with a strong steering committee.[1] An effective steering committee protects you from being blindsided by big risks, minimizes wasted time and rework by a project team, and, critically helps you make better decisions that will save you money and get your revenue stream flowing faster.

Let's say you are a sales executive sponsoring a project that will build a factory to make a new product. Customers have told you that a small change in product characteristics will increase sales. You have no project management or technical background. What you really care about is meeting the commitments that you have made to customers. While the project team is responsible for identifying, evaluating, and recommending alternatives, you still have to be involved in decisions about technology or factory design that affect the things you *do* care about, especially the production schedule. For this example, the new product requires some modifications to the manufacturing process. The change is not huge, but the equipment has never been used quite this way. The feedback from the team is that they need some additional analysis to reduce the technical risk before completing the design. The testing will extend the schedule by three months, which jeopardizes your customer commitments. If the testing is not done, there is a 25 percent chance that you will not meet the customer commitments anyway because the equipment will not work.

What do you do? Do you take the technical risk and go ahead with the planned schedule? After all, there is a chance that everything will work fine. Perhaps there is a work-around that will allow you to still

---

[1]Different names used for steering committees include governance committees, project boards, and decision review boards.

meet customer commitments while the technical group fixes any problems that are encountered. Or, should you contact your customers now and try to negotiate new agreements?

A steering committee is set up to help you work through issues just like these in which you have to make decisions that have important trade-offs such as the balance between risk and reward or cost versus benefit in areas in which you have little subject-matter expertise. In this example, the steering committee, which includes the managers of the project management and technology organizations, would help the project sponsor work through the risks of various alternatives, so that a good decision could be made.

## How to Build a Strong Steering Committee

A few years ago I did research on project steering committees and the practices that made them more or less effective. One of the interesting findings was the variability in steering committee performance project-to-project within the same company. Some are good and some are bad. Here is feedback I got from two people who worked at the same company but on different steering committees and on totally separate projects. The first person said:

> The project sponsor had a strong personality; they downplayed concerns about project risks and pushed the project forward.

This a common problem with steering committees. One person dominates the committee and prevents an open dialogue about project risks or alternative strategies. Needless to say, there was not a good balance between risk and reward on this project. By the way, the problem is not limited to the project sponsor. I have seen steering committees controlled by the technology or engineering executive pushing a solution they believe is best. Sometimes this behavior is the result of someone acting in their best interest rather than the best interest of the company. But usually it is an individual who truly believes they are doing what is best for the company and is not willing to hear feedback to the contrary.

The feedback I got from another person about their experience on a different steering committee at the same company was an interesting contrast.

> The project steering committee was an excellent forum for reaching consensus on the project scope and strategy.

Same company, same expectation for steering committees, yet very different results. A good project sponsor encourages debate and hears all sides before making a decision. The lesson here is that you are not guaranteed good results just because you have a steering committee.

A steering committee is a team, and just like any team, it takes time to understand roles and responsibilities, form relationships, and build the trust needed to have open dialogue. You should view the time and effort required to build a strong team as an investment that will pay off as the project moves through the full life cycle. Team charters, defined roles and responsibilities, and clear delegation of authority are all effective tools for building a strong team. All members of the steering committee are responsible for making it function properly. If the steering committee does not have a charter, for example, you develop a draft to get the process started.

To be effective, the members of the steering committee should have about the same level of authority. Having individuals with the same level of authority helps to avoid the problem of *group-think*, in which the group minimizes conflict and reaches a consensus without discussion of dissenting views. The strong committee is made up of individuals with diverse expertise, access to different information, and distinct perspectives on the best choices for project scope and strategy.

Individuals with less seniority are more likely to keep their opinions to themselves if they disagree with the committee chair. Clients that I work with try as best they can to staff steering committees with peers. Some of the worst steering committees for major investments are chaired by the CEO or the business unit president because nobody is willing to tell them that the project is headed for disaster.

## Who to Include in the Steering Committee

You want to keep the committee as small as possible to make decision making easier but with enough representation to get adequate input on important issues. Decision making gets harder with more people on the committee. It is harder to schedule meetings, it takes longer to update everyone on status, and more people have to give their opinions. On the other hand, you do not want to miss input from stakeholders who can help you reach higher performance on your fundamental objectives.

Some core functions should always be represented on a steering committee (Figure 9.1). One of those is the operator or end user of the asset. They usually have the biggest stake in the decisions that

**Figure 9.1 Core Functions That Should Always Be Represented on a Steering Committee**

determine how the asset will work and what it will do. By far, the most contentious trade-off on capital projects is between asset functionality and capital cost. To minimize capital cost, a business wants to install enough asset functionality to achieve good performance but no more. Spending more to install capability that is not needed is a waste of money. Let's say the project is to purchase, install, and deploy new customer relationship software. The objective is to increase customer retention by increasing the information available to manage and analyze customer activity. Someone has to decide which features the sales force really needs to do the job. The person who has to make the final decision is the project sponsor, not the project manager. The project manager usually does not have the authority to tell operations or the end user no. The steering committee is the forum in which these issues can be debated and resolved.

The steering committee must also include representatives of the technical and project management functions that will support the project. Many project decisions in one form or another are a trade-off between business risk and project risk. For example, the decision to accelerate a schedule to meet a market window is trading the risk of missing a revenue opportunity for the risk of a cost overrun or asset performance shortfall. A decision to cut the capacity of the asset late in the project life cycle because of forecasted lower demand is trading the risk of stranded capital against, again, the risk of cost overruns, schedule overruns, and asset performance shortfalls. Just like the example I started with, the role of the technical and project management representatives is to make sure the trade-off information is reliable and that you understand the consequences of each alternative before making the decision.

Most projects just need three or four members other than the project sponsor to form an effective steering committee. Larger projects that affect multiple businesses will need representation from those organizations. A project that requires financing or that needs to work through a difficult legal issue may need finance and legal representation. You can decide what you need to help with decision making. You can also bring in other functions periodically or on an as-needed basis.

You can hire subject matter experts to help you if your company does not have a technical or project management function. I have worked with several companies that have used experienced executives who have recently retired from large corporations to plug gaps in their experience base very effectively. These grizzled veterans bring a wealth of knowledge and are eager for something to do after they have gotten tired of playing golf or tennis every day.

## Run the Steering Committee Efficiently

A steering committee meets regularly, usually once a month, but very large projects or projects that are not encountering many problems may not need to meet as frequently. The agenda for the meeting usually includes a review of project status and action items, as well as discussion of problems and emerging risks. The committee members make decisions as necessary. However, the steering committee members must also be available if an emergency arises and the project manager needs a decision made on how to handle the problem. The meeting is chaired by the project sponsor, but the project manager is the person who prepares the material and runs much of the meeting.

You can make the meeting more efficient by insisting that the agenda focus on exceptions to the project plan rather than a general update that regurgitates unimportant details, that preread material is prepared and actually reviewed prior to the meeting, that minutes are taken, and that decisions are documented. You want to free up as much time as necessary to talk about the important issues facing the project.

One of the worst behaviors that undermines a steering committee is members not showing up or having a subordinate attend in their stead. Decisions cannot really be made if the right people are not there. You have chosen these people to help you, but they cannot provide input if they are not there. You need to secure their commitment up front.

All members of the steering committee can make it more efficient by not only showing up, but also by supporting the other members, keeping the big picture in mind, and taking the time to understand their point of view. They should also provide input to the agenda prior to the meeting.

## Make Decisions at the Right Level

A project steering committee does not make all project decisions; most are delegated to the project team once the objectives are established. The steering committee makes choices on scope and strategy that are basic to the business case or have a significant trade-off. The steering committee will chose between options for something like asset capacity but will not get involved in the asset design details. Those are left with the project team. In fact, once the main options have been chosen, about midway through the Select stage, the steering committee starts to operate more and more on a manage-by-exception basis. At this point, the steering committee establishes tolerances for outcomes such as cost growth. For example, the steering committee may say that as long as capital costs are forecasted to stay within 10 percent of the budget, the project manager can decide how best to respond to problems. However, when problems emerge that will cause costs to go over the tolerance, the project manager must get steering committee approval on any corrective action. Managing by exception reduces the burden on the executives and managers on the steering committee.

Project steering committees do not make the final stage-gate decision. Stage-gate decisions are typically reserved for an investment committee of executives who have a more objective view of the project's merits. The investment committee may be led by the executive I described in the project sponsor chapter who has oversight responsibility for the capital in the business. Giving the investment committee final stage-gate decision authority provides for checks and balances on the project sponsor. The investment committee also includes portfolio management objectives in their decision making. They might rank the project against other opportunities based on criteria such as alignment with corporate strategy, potential return on investment, and diversification potential.

## Do Not Dilute Project Sponsor Accountability

A danger with any steering committee is diluted accountability for the success of the project. It is easy for steering committee members to blame one another if something is wrong or if final decision-making authority is not clear.

The project sponsor is the main driver of the project. A project is steered by guiding and approving objectives, choosing which options for scope and strategy best satisfy the defined business objectives, and giving direction on how to respond to emerging risks that threaten the project. In other words, steering means setting the destination, deciding the best way to get there, and figuring out what to do if the project drifts off course. The project sponsor owns the business case and is accountable for business outcomes; therefore, they get final decision authority when the committee cannot reach consensus. However, there needs be a mechanism for escalating issues if other committee members believe the project sponsor is making decisions that significantly increase project risk unnecessarily. This is equivalent to the brake pedal a driving teacher has on their side of the car so that

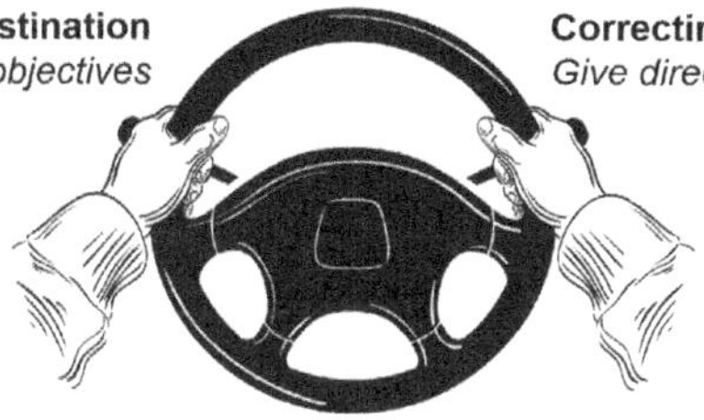

**Selecting the Best Route**
*Choose scope and strategy options
that satisfy business objectives*

**Setting the Destination**                    **Correcting When Drifting Off Course**
*Guide and approve objectives*                 *Give direction for responding to risks*

**Figure 9.2  The Project Sponsor Is the Main Driver of the Project**

they can pump the brakes before the car goes over a cliff. (See Figure 9.2.)

A more senior executive needs to get involved when a disagreement cannot be resolved at the steering committee level. Usually the disagreement is between the project sponsor and technical or project management function about project risk. The manager is probably concerned the project sponsor is refusing to recognize a significant project risk that jeopardizes the overall business case. Remember that the project management organization is responsible for delivering a quality asset, on time, and on budget. I have seen many times where the business reason for taking the project risk was forgotten and the project manager was blamed for not delivering when the project had poor results.

One engineering manager described how the escalation process works at their company:

> When there are issues that we cannot agree on, the project sponsor and I meet with the senior business leader to get resolution. Sometimes the business leader decides to accept the risk to the business case, but the risk is documented and transparent to all.

An essential part of the process is what happens next:

> My job then is to ensure the project team is aligned and focused on doing their best to achieve the targets.

Because the risk is understood and transparent, the project
manager is able to say to the project team that management
understands and accepts the risk. The team is then able to align around
that goal and develop strategies that mitigate the risk and plan for the
uncertainties. Without management's acknowledgment of the risk, a
team can become demoralized and worry much more about getting
blamed than figuring out ways to meet the challenge.

Sometimes an informal escalation process is already in place at a
company. Long-tenured technical and project professionals who have
strong credibility with the businesses or corporate executives are able
get an audience when necessary. However, you should not rely on
someone taking the risk to stick their neck out when something
concerns them. Some of my clients have established an escalation
process to allow intervention as early as possible. The process is really
just instruction for what someone should do if they believe a problem
needs to be raised to the next level of management.

You will not have to rely on an escalation process if the culture at
your company is to be *surprise averse* rather than *risk averse*. People
should be able to freely raise concerns and have a debate as decisions
are made. You do not want to hear about problems after there is
nothing you can do about them. You can start modeling the behavior
by actively encouraging dialogue. Constructive tension between
functions with different points of view produces better projects.

# 10 Risk Management: A Mechanism to Understand Project Risk and Decide What to Do

Risk management is an important tool executives have at their disposal for understanding, monitoring, and making decisions about *individual* project risks. A good definition of an individual risk is "an uncertain event that, if it occurs, has a positive or negative effect on one or more objectives."[1] Risk management is the process of identifying individual risks, understanding and analyzing them, and then managing them by doing something about them. Examples of individual risks include bad weather, a shortage of experienced software engineers, an earthquake, or an economic recession. The types of risks executives and project sponsors care about are those that threaten the project's business objectives.[2] The risk of a shortage of experienced software engineers is only interesting to an executive if the shortage is a real threat to the project's business objectives.

In this chapter, I describe how to get the most value from risk management. Often risk management is not used to its full potential. Sometimes not enough discipline is applied. Sometimes there is too much focus on the minutiae. When this happens, the executives and project team miss an opportunity to align on the important risks and decide on the best course of action to manage those risks.

Too often the communication between the business and the project team about risk is problematic. Part of the difficulty is that

---

[1]Project Management Institute, *A Guide to the Project Management Body of Knowledge*, 5th ed. (Newtown Square, PA: Project Management Institute, 2013).
[2]A more accurate statement would be to say that risks present both opportunities and threats to business objectives. Risks are uncertainties that can turn out favorably or unfavorably. For example, the cost to purchase land for a new building could be more or less than expected. If the cost is less than expected, the business might want to build a bigger building rather than just pocketing the savings. To simplify the discussion, I am going to focus on mainly risks that are threats to objectives, but anything I describe can also be applied to opportunities.

both parties have different views on project risk. Project teams view individual project risks only as threats to cost, schedule, and asset performance predictability—the areas the team typically measures. Executives often have a broader view. They view project risks as a means to achieve a fundamental business objective such as making money. Project teams are not stupid, however. Businesses oftentimes equate risk management with risk elimination, and any overrun means the project manager did a bad job managing risk. Risk management dampens risk, but does not eliminate it unless the risk is avoided altogether. Consequently, both parties end up being wary of each other and not trusting each other's motives, hardly the ingredients for a productive partnership.

I want to start with a short case study on how risk management enabled collaboration between the business and the project team and yielded the exact project strategy the business wanted. This example shows how risk management can cut through the fog and produce a good result for everyone. I was part of the IPA evaluation team that supported this project by quantifying schedule risk and investigating different risk mitigation strategies.

The business would be able to enter into some favorable long-term supply agreements if the project were completed before the company's competitors could lock in their own deals. The business knew that competitors were forming plans for their own projects. The main challenge was that the business wanted to construct a facility in 14 months that would normally take 25 months to build, a full 11 months faster. Our database showed that only 1 in 20 similar projects were able to finish construction that quickly, not very good odds of success. Furthermore, projects such as this one with very aggressive targets risk ending up in worse shape than if they had just set an average target in the first place. About a quarter of the projects in our database that tried to go this fast ended up not only overrunning their aggressive targets but also having longer than average schedule durations! The risks taken to go fast and the mistakes made in the haste can lead to catastrophic failure.

Understanding that the chance of hitting the schedule target was low, the team used a risk management process that produced several very good mitigation strategies, all of which required spending extra money. First, the project paid a premium to hire a contractor who had experience building this type of facility. The team also hired extra owner staff, paid to expedite equipment delivery, and planned for construction overtime. These risk mitigation strategies added an extra 50 percent to the cost of building the facility. Even after implementing the strategies, there was still only a 30 percent chance the project would be finished on time.

This next part is the most important. Working through the schedule risk using the risk management process in a collaborative, transparent way meant the executives understood the cost of the risk mitigation and understood the residual risk as they made their decision, which was to move forward with the risk mitigation strategies. The business objective was to sign supply contracts before their competitor did; the business accepted the cost of the mitigation and the remaining 70 percent chance of slip for the potential payoff. The other option was to change the business objective to be first, back off the schedule target, and hope the competition did not finish before they did.

The project ended up finishing in 16 months, after a two-month delay caused by a construction error that was not caught until the facility was put into service. This is a very common problem on fast projects. Half of the projects in our database that went as fast as this project did had significant problems during startup. In the end, the business was satisfied with the result. The asset was still built seven months faster than the average and beat the competition to the market.

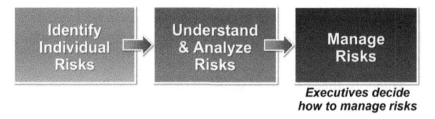

Figure 10.1  Main Elements of a Risk Management Process

## Risk Management: Identify, Analyze, and Manage Individual Risks

As I defined earlier, risk management is the process of identifying individual risks, understanding and analyzing them, and then managing them by doing something about them. I am not going to go into the details of how risks are identified, understood, and analyzed, but I do want to discuss how risks are managed (see Figure 10.1).

Executives decide how specific risks are managed, so you need to understand your options. Let's use a new technology example again to explore the different ways a risk could be managed. In this example, a project is building a factory using an innovative technology that has not yet been proved in commercial use. The risk is that the technology will not work as well as expected, and the factory won't be able to make the product as fast as expected to meet customer requirements. This risk could be managed using one or some combination of the methods shown in Table 10.1.

The best course of action depends on a number of factors, including the importance of the new technology to the business objectives, the probability that the risk will occur, the consequences of occurrence, and the cost to mitigate it. For example, the business could just avoid the risk if the technology is not a core objective. The technology needed to reduce operating costs may be nice to have but not absolutely necessary. The project will still make money even if the tried-and-true technology is used. The business might just decide to

## Table 10.1 Methods for Managing Risks

| Method to Manage the Risk | Possible Response |
| --- | --- |
| Avoid | Switch to a tried-and-true technology and eliminate the innovation. |
| Hedge | Look for opportunities to purchase the product from another supplier to make up any production gap from the new technology. |
| Mitigate—lower the chance of occurrence | Delay the project and perform more pilot testing to reduce technical risk. |
| Mitigate the effect | Install extra production capacity, so that even if it operates below total capacity, there is enough to meet demand. |
| Accept the risk | Add money to the capital cost budget and time to schedule to fix the problem if it occurs. |

avoid the risk altogether in this case. However, if the business goal is to undercut the prices of the company's competition to take market share, the technology may be integral to the project's justification.

If the risk cannot be avoided, some combination of risk mitigation strategies may be used to reduce risk, depending on the benefit of the strategies versus their cost. The business may just decide to accept the risk if the risk mitigation strategies do not provide enough value. If the business accepts the risk, they will add contingency to the cost and schedule to provide some protection against the risk if it occurs. In this particular case, the strategy of accepting the risk of significantly new technology rarely actually works because the risk is often underestimated. When this happens, you may inadvertently end up with a large-scale pilot plant. An endemic problem that I will discuss later in the chapter is the tendency to significantly underestimate the effect of project risks.

These options for managing risks are the levers executives pull to shape project strategy in the way they believe is best for achieving the project's business objectives. They have to work closely with the project team to make good decisions on which levers to pull. This back-and-forth produces the real benefit of opening the lines of communication and keeping them open.

## Practices for Getting the Most from Risk Management

Risk management starts in the Assess stage as the project frame is being developed. It is critical to identify uncertainties and risks early enough to guide basic strategy development. In Chapter 5, I shared the example of a business needing different options for the size of a factory because the demand forecast was highly uncertain. The business faced the risk of building a plant that was too big if demand turned out to be lower than expected and the risk of building a plant that was too small if demand was higher than expected. The risk management process is the perfect mechanism for communicating the uncertainty and risk to the project team so that they understand it and start thinking of alternative strategies for managing the risk.

Cast a wide net when thinking about risk. Often risk management focuses too much on one source of risk, usually technical and project execution risks. For example, a project execution risk could be that *vendor-supplied data are late* or *labor productivity is worse than expected.* Executives do not focus enough on commercial risks, such as *the customer contract is delayed* or *financing from lenders is more expensive than expected.* Technical and project execution risks are important, but so are economic, market, and commercial risks. In fact, these are the risks that may prompt major changes in the project scope and strategy. Failure to get financing for an affordable rate may lead to canceling the project. Delays in the customer contract may lead to a change in product mix that, in turn, requires a redesign of the equipment.

Including all types of risks keeps the lines of communication open, especially from the executives and project sponsors to the project team.

Keeping the risk register current is a constant challenge. One of the problems with risk management is that the discipline to keep the risk register current decreases as the project workload increases. To be effective, the risk register needs to be updated on a regular basis, with risks added, dropped, or modified as needed. The burden of keeping the register current can be reduced by only including risks that are severe or opportunistic enough to monitor. Executives in the steering and investment committees can help provide the discipline by asking to see the risk register on a regular basis.

## Scrutinize Risks to Decide Whether They Are Worth Taking

Risks are only important if they threaten an objective you care about. As a silly example, the potential for damaging earthquakes in California is certainly a risk, but it is only a project risk if the asset is being built in California or perhaps if one of the main suppliers is located in California. Risks can creep into projects for objectives that are not that important to the business. I have seen the risk register used very effectively to winnow out scope that is a low priority to the business. Table 10.2 shows an entry in a simple risk register that describes the risk and the severity of the risk.

**Table 10.2  Example Entry of a Risk Register**

| Risk | Severity | Response/ Action Plan |
|---|---|---|
| Problems refurbishing equipment delay the turnaround | *High:* Possible three-day delay of factory shutdown | To be decided |

In this case, the risk is high because the project was expanding an existing factory. Oftentimes, the work to finish a project must be done when the factory is *shut down* so that the construction crews can get access to all the equipment and to do the work safely. A business is not making any money when the factory is shut down, so the goal is to get the work done as quickly as possible. For this factory, every day the factory was shut down meant a loss of $1.25 million in revenue.

The project sponsor learned about the risk when reviewing the risk register with the project team. The equipment that was being refurbished was something that operations requested to make the equipment more reliable, but the effect of the risk was not as important to the business as getting the factory back up and running as soon as possible. The risk was avoided by removing the scope of work from the project. As this example illustrates, any discussion about the causes of risks can be a very effective tool for gaining alignment on the existence of risks and, in turn, objectives and priorities, with executives and other influential stakeholders.

## Understand That the Estimate of the Risk Is Probably Too Low

Estimates of risks, both the probability of occurrence and consequence, are much more likely to be underestimated than overestimated. A recent study we did compared the actual cost of labor shortages and weather delays to project team estimates when the event occurred.[3] The study showed that teams routinely underestimated costs by two or three times, meaning that if the team estimated the effect of a risk at $250,000, the actual cost was more like $500,000 to $750,000. The project teams that did these estimates were staffed with experienced project professionals and had access to sophisticated

---

[3]Pete Thomas and Alex Ogilvie, "Quantifying the Real Effects of Project Risk" (annual meeting of the Cost Engineering Committee, IPA, Ashburn, VA, 2015).

estimating tools, yet they still got it wrong. The problem is that the risks that affect one area ripple through capital projects in ways that are difficult to foresee.

The tendency to underestimate risks does not mean risk management is a waste of time. It does mean you have to be careful when a project team puts in front of you what seems to be a very precise estimate of the probability a risk will occur, and the cost if it does occur. You should probe around to understand how the estimate was developed and ask the team how confident they are about the level of uncertainty in the estimate. You can ask people outside the team what they think about the risk. Most important, you should explore all options for avoiding the risk before approving risk mitigation strategies or accepting the risk.

## Be Careful with Making Late Changes in Response to Business Risk

Business risks are uncertainties that may cause a change in project scope or strategy to keep the business case viable. Say an economic slowdown reduces the cash a business has available to pay for a project. The business may respond to this risk by looking for ways to cut project costs or slow down project spending. In addition to economic conditions, competitor and customer actions are business risks. A competitor announcing that it has a superior technology may undercut the justification for a project. An unexpected shift in customer preferences may require the business to change its products. In turn, these events may cause the business to make changes to asset functionality, project strategy, and project timing to keep the investment profitable.

By far, the most common response to business risks is to cut capital cost. This can take many forms. The project scope can be reduced or the team can look for ways to improve design and construction productivity. Another strategy is to relax the schedule targets to reduce project risk. Going back to the example at the beginning of this chapter, say the market changed and the business value from being first to sign supply agreements had dropped significantly. The business, if they did not cancel the project, would have slowed the project down to cut costs.

The problem with cost reductions is that the estimated reductions are often an illusion unless there is real scope reduction. To truly cut scope means the business has to give up something it wanted originally. For example, if you wanted to build in some extra capacity to expand later, that option may have to go away. Yes, a project team can sharpen the pencil and try to ferret out inefficiency, but if a project team says they can reduce the project cost by more than 5 percent without giving up something you wanted, the team is either scared to tell you the truth or they have made a mistake developing the cost estimate.

Making changes after starting the Define stage may not actually save you as much money as expected even if you cut scope. When a project enters the Define stage, the work branches off into parallel paths, making it difficult to see all the adjustments that have to be made in response to the change. Just like I discussed earlier, the cost of the change is usually underestimated by 2.5 times![4]

You should carefully weigh changes in response to business risk, starting in the Define stage. Changes in the execution stage are even more disruptive and should only be made as a last resort. Making changes during execution usually means tearing out concrete and moving equipment that has already been installed.

---

[4]Edward Merrow and Laura Mayo, "The Effects of Changes Late in Front-End Loading" (annual meeting of the Industry Benchmarking Conference, IPA, March 2005).

## Strong Risk Management Does Not Substitute for Strong Project Definition

The overall riskiness of a project with weak definition can still be high even if the project has taken a detailed approach to risk management. You cannot manage risks you do not know about, sometimes referred to as *unknown unknowns.* Project definition activities change *unknown unknowns* into *known unknowns*, which are risks you can manage. For example, a project team that conducts a labor survey, a standard project definition activity, might find out that there is a potential for a construction labor shortage in the project's location. The survey shows that a high number of projects are planning to build in that area in the same time period. The work will soak up much of the skilled labor in the area. Without the survey, the project team would have been oblivious to the risk (an unknown unknown). Because of the survey, the team can manage the risk in any number of ways. They could delay the project to avoid the risk, they could plan to pay a higher wage to attract labor to their project to mitigate the risk, or they could accept the risk after deciding it will not have much of an impact on the project.

Strong project definition is the best risk management tool. Remember that projects with weak definition have much more volatile results than projects with strong definition. One in four projects with weak definition erodes 50 percent or more value from cost and schedule overruns and technical problems. Only 1 in 10 projects with strong definition has the same outcome. Project definition tasks, such as labor surveys, technical studies, site surveys, vendor prequalification assessments, safety studies, and the like, systemically discover the uncertainties that are lurking out there before they creep up and get you from behind.

Strong definition, coupled with an integrated team that is aligned around the objectives and that has all the expertise needed to identify risks, can stop many risks in their tracks by eliminating the uncertainty behind them. Take for example a software project that is developing a new application that will interface with an existing database. Having a database administrator who knows the structure and security requirements of the existing database will prevent the application developer from designing an interface that creates "bad" (incorrectly formatted) data that does not easily integrate into the existing database.

# 11 Approve, Recycle, Cancel, or Hold

**Making Good Stage-Gate Decisions**

S tage-gates are checkpoints built into the project delivery process that give executives the opportunity to review the merits of a capital project to decide whether money should be invested in pursuing an opportunity or solving a problem. Let me give you a very simple example to illustrate their purpose. Let's say the furniture in an office building is worn and outdated. The office manager proposes to replace all the furniture with a more modern design, especially getting the height-adjustable desks that everybody wants now. However, the owner of the business knows that the office lease is up in three years and the office will probably move to a new location. Spending money on new furniture now would be a waste of money. The owner does not know the layout of the new office building. The company might even get rid of offices altogether and go with an open-concept design. In this case, the best course of action is to live with the current furniture and only replace what is broken.

The owner is able to stop the proposal before much time and effort is spent developing the idea if the business has a requirement that all proposals must be reviewed early. This review—or *gate*—prevents ideas that should never get approved from gaining momentum. Without the requirement, the owner may not see the proposal until after the office manager has formed a committee to decide on the kind of furniture that should be purchased, has gotten three quotes from suppliers, and has all the paperwork ready for the owner's signature. You will still be able to cancel the project at this point but time has been wasted and now your staff is disappointed that they are not getting the new furniture. They might even accuse you of being indifferent to their health because they cannot get those adjustable desks where they can stand up and do their work!

Operating the stage-gates for capital projects is usually more complex than this example, but it illustrates the key point that the stage-gates are there to ensure that only the highest-priority projects are funded and that spending on projects that will ultimately not go forward is stopped at the earliest possible time.

## Capital Investment Decisions Are Made at the Stage-Gates

The focus of this chapter is on the executives who are making the investment decision as opposed to the executives who are proposing capital projects for their business. For example, a business general manager wants to increase margins by installing some equipment that uses less energy. That executive has to get approval from more senior executives to get the capital. To make funding decisions, a committee of senior executives will review the business case, focusing on a core set of questions to judge the merits of the project:

- Are the project's objectives aligned with the corporate and business strategic goals?
- Does the project have a high enough expected return on investment?
- Can the business afford the investment?
- Is the timing for the investment acceptable?
- Is the project a higher priority than other investment alternatives that are competing for the same scarce capital and people resources?

These questions help the investment committee decide whether the project is a good use of capital. A company usually only has so much capital to invest. Senior, usually corporate, executives must decide how to allocate capital to the company's various business units. Stage-gates enable senior executives to build a portfolio of projects that support and advance operational and growth strategies by only allowing the highest-priority projects to move forward.

Let's say a business has the choice to expand in Asia or in Europe. The stage-gate process is the platform for deciding which project will

Start       GATE 1           GATE 2           GATE 3           Handover
                                             Authorization

**Figure 11.1  Stage-Gate Project Development and Delivery Process**

deliver the highest value back to the business. The lower-value project is stopped early in the process, say after the Assess or Select gates, while the higher-value project is allowed to proceed.

## Three Gates Provide Adequate Control

The typical stage-gate system has a total of three gates. The final investment decision is made at Gate 3, the last gate before a project starts execution. (See Figure 11.1.)

I will talk about the purpose of each gate more in a minute, but first I want to show how the gates allow executives to minimize the amount of money spent to develop a project before it could be canceled. Table 11.1 shows how much money is typically needed to complete each of the first three stages of the project life cycle. The numbers in the table are the averages for projects in IPA's databases. There are many factors that could increase or decrease the money needed for each stage. For example, the commitment in Define could

**Table 11.1  Typical Financial Commitment for Each Stage**

| Project Stage | Average Percentage of Total Budget to Complete the Stage | Amount Needed for a $10 Million Project | Cumulative Total |
|---|---|---|---|
| Assess | 0.5% | $50,000 | $50,000 |
| Select | 1.5% | $150,000 | $200,000 |
| Define | 3.0% | $300,000 | $500,000 |
| Execute | 95.0% | $9,500,000 | $10,000,000 |

be higher if a project orders equipment or supplies with long delivery times. However, the overall finding that the financial commitment for the next stage escalates at each gate still holds true. The money for the Select stage is about *three times* the budget for the Assess stage. And completing the Define stage will cost twice as much as completing Select. It is easy to see why stopping nonviable projects early is important. The further the project gets in its life cycle, the more costs are sunk—and thus lost—if the project is canceled.

Deciding to cancel a project or change direction when only $50,000 has been spent to complete the Assess stage is much better than spending ten times that amount and pulling the plug at the end of the Define stage. Companies with weak or nonexistent gates at the end of Assess and Select waste money by allowing projects to go down the wrong path before making adjustments.

Sometimes the problem is more than financial. Canceling a project just before authorization may damage the business's reputation with shareholders, the financial community, partners, and other external stakeholders. For example, a major investment may be viewed by the stock analysts as critical to a company's long-term financial success. They may downgrade their assessment of the company's prospects if the project they believed was going to be authorized is canceled. It is better to weed out the projects that are not going to make it before expectations are set.

Executives who wait too long to stop projects can end up like those poor frogs that are supposedly boiled alive in a pot when the heat is turned up slowly. The frog does not know to jump because it does not notice the increase in temperature until it is too late. For executives, the money spent in project definition can grow so large that canceling the project and generating a large chunk of sunk costs can be a very difficult decision to make. And, because forward-going economics are used to make investment decisions, the sunk costs do not even figure into the decision. A project that has purchased some equipment early without the ability to cancel the order may simply be viable because so much money has already been spent. Executives needed to intervene before the financial commitment was made.

## The Business Question Asked and Answered at Each Stage-Gate

Many activities occur at each stage-gate, but from a business perspective, the most important question that needs to be asked and answered at each stage-gate is: *Does the possible value from this opportunity justify spending the money to complete the next stage of the process?* The same basic question is asked at each stage-gate, but as the project progresses from Gate 1 to Gate 3, the confidence executives have in their decision increases, provided the process and the stage-gates are being operated correctly. Figure 11.2 shows how the question changes from Gate 1 to Gate 3.

The answer changes from "I think so" at Gate 1 to "I am confident it is" by Gate 3. At Gate 1, there is not enough certainty in the estimates underpinning the business case to decide anything other than that the project has enough *potential* value to continue. For example, the capital cost estimate prepared for Gate 1 is usually highly uncertain because there is very little scope and planning definition. As discussed in Chapter 8, the cost estimate prepared at the Assess gate can swing

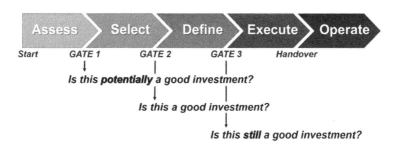

**Figure 11.2 The Key Business Questions Asked and Answered at Each Stage-Gate**

widely, but let's assume the estimate has a range from minus 50 percent to plus 50 percent, meaning that a $5 million estimate prepared at the end of Assess could end up costing anywhere from $2.5 million to $7.5 million. Few executives should be willing to make a final investment decision on a project with a cost that could swing by so much. There is also great uncertainty in the other key inputs to the investment analysis: project schedule, asset technical performance, and fixed and variable operating costs. Unless the investment analysis shows that the business case is robust at higher costs or other worst-case scenarios, the project should die here or be reworked in the Assess stage. If the economics are robust, the executives allow the project to move forward for further development.

I refer to Gate 2 as the business authorization gate. By Gate 2, the stage-gate process is designed to reduce the uncertainty in the business case to a level that executives can judge the attractiveness of the business case with reasonable confidence. There is still considerable work to do in the Define stage, and the project estimates at Gate 2 still have a moderate level of uncertainty, but unless something major changes or mistakes were made, the estimates should be robust enough that the project is very likely to receive full funds approval. A project system is working well if very few projects are canceled at Gate 3.

The final investment decision is made at Gate 3. The work in Define is done to verify that the business case is solid and to prevent the project from falling apart as it moves into Execute.


## Use Your Early Stage-Gates Better

Gates 1 and 2 are often conducted with less rigor and discipline than Gate 3. The heightened focus on Gate 3 is understandable considering the difference in financial commitment, but this is shortsighted. Projects that start off with a weak frame or unclear objectives usually have to go back and rework those issues. Projects with marginal business cases rarely get stronger as they move through the project life cycle. As I showed in Chapter 8, capital costs tend to increase and risks tend to be more visible, putting downward pressure on the expected return on investment.

Do not wait until the authorization decision before giving the project a thorough evaluation. You are spending too much money and missing the best time to take action.

## Four Choices for the Stage-Gate Decision

*Approve, recycle, cancel,* and *hold* are the four potential outcomes for the investment committee decision. (See Figure 11.3.) Consider an executive committee that includes the president, chief financial officer, and vice president of operations of a paper company reviewing the business case for a project that has reached Gate 2. The project is to expand one of their paper mills. The committee can approve the project to move into the Define stage if they are satisfied with the business case. They can recycle the project back to the Select stage if they want the team to consider other options for the expansion or they are not satisfied with the project team's work. About 15 percent of all projects are recycled at a stage-gate. Recycle is not uncommon if the business case is near the minimum return on investment or the cost is close to the budget limit. However, too many projects with incomplete

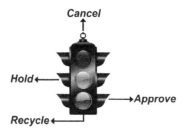

**Figure 11.3 The Four Potential Outcomes from the Stage-Gate Decision**

work are not recycled. Instead, they are allowed to pass through the gate. Too often project sponsors and project managers are not held accountable for the quality of their work in preparation for the stage-gate. I will discuss later how this undermines the effectiveness of the stage-gates.

The committee can cancel the project outright if they conclude that the business case is weak and there is little chance it can be improved. Last, they can put the project on hold if the timing of the project is not right. For this project, although the business case meets the minimum return on investment, the committee decides to put the project on hold. There are some early signs of an economic slowdown, and the executives do not think it is prudent to commit to the project until the forecasts are better. The project team is told to tie up any loose ends so that the project can be easily restarted if they decide to move forward in six months.

## Information Used in an Investment Decision

Figure 11.4 shows the typical contents of a project's business case. These elements of the business case, combined with the dialogue during the stage-gate meeting, provide the information executives need to make the investment decision.

The business case, which is summarized in a few pages or presentation slides, is just the tip of a pyramid of underlying data and

| 🔍 Business Case Contents | |
| --- | --- |
| Executive Summary | Justification |
| Background | Scope Overview |
| Objectives | Investment Analysis |
| *(Targets, Constraints, Priorities)* | |

**Figure 11.4  Typical Contents of a Business Case**

analysis. Just to give you an idea of the work required, a project team may have to prepare as many as 10 separate deliverables for a Gate 1 meeting and as many as 30 for a Gate 3 meeting for a large project. The deliverables include a master schedule, technical design details, organization charts, cost estimates, and project execution plans. Even a small project will have about 15 different work items to complete for authorization. Doing all this work is why projects spend so much money and take so much time doing project definition.

Executives don't see all the details at each gate—nor should they— but they will probably be sorry if those details are not there. The work required for each gate is not arbitrary. It is calibrated to the decision being made. For example, the master schedule for a $1 million project probably only needs about five milestone activities to be detailed enough for the Gate 1 decision. By the time it gets to Gate 2, we need more schedule detail because the stakes are much higher. The master schedule at Gate 2 should be developed using a more sophisticated method and should contain about 250 activities to capture the full project scope of work, to provide enough confidence that the schedule estimate is reasonably accurate, and to identify any major risks that may prevent the schedule from being achieved. The quality of the schedule and the other Select stage deliverables is key for getting a reliable cost estimate at the Select gate.

## Rules for Strong Gates

Investment committee decision making is made much easier and more effective if a company establishes a set of rules for the stage-gates. Those rules include:

- The stage-gates are the same for all projects and businesses.
- Each gate has standard deliverables.
- The deliverables are assessed for completeness and quality.
- There are consequences for noncompliance.

The first two rules establish a common basis for making investment decisions at each gate. The rules mean that all projects have to complete a certain amount of work before they can pass through a gate. This supports investment decision making for single projects but also establishes the consistency needed to make good portfolio decisions.

Portfolio decisions have to be made on a level playing field to be fair. Let's say an investment committee is considering two $1 million projects from different business units, and the company can only fund one of the projects. For this example, the expected value for each project presented to the investment committee is identical at $750,000 NPV. The first requirement for choosing is that the return on investment calculation is done in the same way. If not, one project may appear to be more valuable just because a different method was used. A bigger problem, however, is that the economics of projects with weak definition are usually inflated relative to projects with strong definition. Said a different way, projects with weak definition will typically appear to have better economics than projects with strong definition—at least initially.

In Chapter 7, I showed that projects with weak definition at authorization erode about 25 percent of their expected value from cost and schedule growth and asset performance shortfalls. Projects with strong definition deliver the promised value. If these two projects follow form, the project with weak definition will only deliver $562,000 in NPV while other project will deliver the promised $750,000. (See Figure 11.5.)

Establishing the requirement that most—if not all—projects reach strong definition at each gate[1] eliminates a source of bias that causes a

---

[1] I discuss the issue of how the investment committee should approach granting exceptions from the stage-gate requirements for some projects at the end of the chapter.

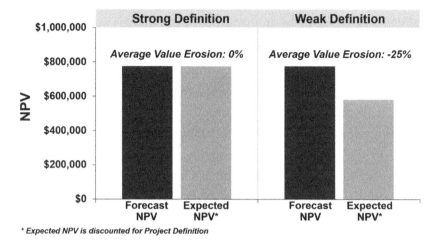

**Figure 11.5 Expected Value Is Higher When Project Definition Is Weak**

company to systematically select projects that overstate the expected value of the investment over projects that have a more accurate assessment. On a single project, value erosion of 25 percent may not mean much, but over time, the bias in the system will lead to significantly lower shareholder value generated from capital projects.

## Account for Human Nature

The rules for checking deliverables for completeness and quality and having consequences for noncompliance are there to address the weaknesses of human nature and human decision making. Someone has to check the quality of the information used to develop the business case for accuracy and completeness. Project sponsors or project managers will not always be forthcoming about or fully understand the uncertainty and risk in a business case. The reasons this happens range from blatant self-interest, wishful thinking, not including the correct stakeholders, to just plain ignorance. I will discuss this more a bit later, but the reality is that sometimes the business case reviewed by an investment committee is not worth the cost of the paper it is printed on.

Here is an extreme but real example of how the project sponsor and technology leader buried the risk of a project strategy, hiding it from the investment committee. The sponsor and technology leader came up with a strategy for building a low-cost facility in the United States by copying the engineering design from a recently built plant in China. Copying the design would save about 10 percent of the total project cost. Without the savings, the business case was marginal. The project team, however, quickly uncovered some issues that meant the design could not be copied directly from the plant located in China, and thus the savings targets would not be realized. Rather than canceling the project, the project sponsor and technology leader directed the project team to find other ways of cutting the cost and pushed the project through at the original estimate. Unfortunately, the alternatives the team came up with actually made the situation worse, and the project was a complete disaster. The project was 18 months late and costs grew more than 70 percent before it started production. Although the new plant is up and running, it can only produce at 65 percent of its total capacity. The project destroyed all invested capital and more. The executives involved faced the consequences of this failed project: The business sponsor was fired, and the technology leader was forced into early retirement.

As I mentioned, there are several reasons project sponsors or project managers bury the risk when presenting information to the investment committee. A cynic may say that self-interest is the cause for this behavior. For project sponsors, capital is a tool for building a larger, more profitable business. The managers of growing businesses are usually paid more and promoted into better jobs. A project manager without a project might be unemployed. A more positive person might say that the behavior is just an outgrowth of our nature to underestimate the probability of future negative events. Sometimes the problem is that the project sponsor or project manager is blissfully unaware of the risks because of weak project definition or the lack of experience. In my example, the sponsor and technology executive both truly believed they were doing the right thing for the company. In the end, the reason that uncertainties and risks are downplayed does not matter too much, but executives must recognize that it does happen occasionally.

Smart executives seek out independent input on project risk as they are making investment decisions. This may not be always necessary on small projects or in smaller businesses. The executive or group making the investment decision may be close to the project and already understand the strengths and weaknesses of the business case. Of course, those executives have to be careful they are not viewing the project with rose-tinted glasses because they are too close to the project to view it objectively.

## Get Some Assurance

The term *project assurance* describes a whole set of activities that are done to evaluate the entire project or just one aspect. The primary goal of assurance is to identify risk, so that executives can decide what to do about it. For example, a technology review may find that the technology the team has selected is not as robust as the team believes and that the asset may not be able to do what the business expects. An independent review of the cost estimate prepared by the project team is another example of an assurance review.

Two important conditions need to be met to make assurance effective. First, the work must be done by people who are independent of the project team. Countless behavioral studies have shown that we, humans, as a whole are incapable of making honest assessments on the strengths and weaknesses of our own skills or work. IPA has done its own work that confirms that project teams, like the rest of us, are indeed subject to the same biases.[2] Many IPA clients, especially for smaller projects, use self-assessment checklists as a form of assurance. The checklists require the project team to judge the completeness of their work in multiple areas. For example, the checklist will ask teams to rate the completeness of multiple aspects of the technical design and project planning. Any gaps the team identifies cause them to go back and complete the work. However, project teams routinely overstate the quality of their work on these checklists. The problem is that they give themselves partial credit or dismiss gaps that they do not believe create any risk. Project histories show that partially done is not actually done and that sometimes those gaps lead to unexpected problems.

A recent example of this was a project in which the commercial team was negotiating an agreement with a joint-venture partner that was almost (but not quite) final when the project team was formed. The project team began developing the scope of work but was unable to make much progress because the partner would not make any commitments on what it would do as part of the capital project. Consequently, the business was paying for a project team that was not able to accomplish much. We learn this type of lesson all the time. It is dangerous to proceed based on assumptions rather than completed work (in this case, signed commercial agreements).

The investment committees must receive the assurance feedback directly without it being filtered by the project sponsor or project manager. I am always amazed by companies that go through great effort to perform multiple assurance activities, but then do not give the results to the investment committee. In this example, the project's risks were well known by the project manager and his boss, the head of the project management group. IPA also did a project evaluation that

---

[2]Cathy B. Barshop and Gob Juntima, "Self-Assessment Tools—Are They Worth Your Time?" (annual meeting of the Industry Benchmarking Conference, IPA, March 2007).

clearly showed there was a low probability that the cost and schedule targets would be achieved. However, the investment committee never got the feedback or IPA's report because there was no avenue to receive the information unless the executives presenting the business case decided to provide it.

Giving the person who did the assurance or the executive responsible for the assurance the opportunity to provide their feedback directly is the easiest way for investment committees to get the information they need.

### Hold People Accountable

You have an accountability problem if your project sponsor or project managers are routinely overstating benefits or understating risks in the business case. Either there are no consequences for the behavior or there are incentives to cheat.

The best way to get the right behaviors from project sponsors and project managers is to stop projects that have not done the work from going through the gate. The goal for assurance is to find the big problems. It cannot find or fix every problem on a project, especially if the overall quality of the deliverables is poor. There are just too many problems to fix, and some will be missed.

### The Slippery Slope of Granting Exceptions to Stage-Gate Deliverables

Inevitably, the investment committee will be faced with a decision of whether to allow a project to move through a gate even though one of the required deliverables is not complete. For example, let's say a company's process requires that any project involving a joint venture partner must have at least a memorandum of understanding (MOU) with that partner before the project is allowed past Gate 2. The MOU outlines the terms of the business deal and how the joint venture will operate. There is a much higher chance the deal will fall apart without the MOU in place before starting Define. If that happens, the money spent in Define is wasted. For whatever reason, the MOU is not ready at the Gate 2 meeting. The problem is that putting the project on hold until the MOU is signed will cause the project to lose momentum, and, if the delay is long enough, you might even lose some key members of the project team. What do you do? Do you allow the project to go forward or do you shut it down?

Investment committees have to be very careful about their decision even if the decision for that specific project is not that difficult. Say the MOU is being held up on a small detail and really does not present much risk. However, by granting the exception, it will be more difficult to say no to the next project that asks for an exception. Grant the exception to enough projects and the requirement, which is important, becomes unenforceable.

For smaller companies, this may be not much of a problem because it is easy to remember why exceptions were granted and explain to the next team why they are not getting a pass.

Negotiating the slippery slope of exceptions is much more difficult for larger companies. The default position should be that exceptions are only granted in rare cases. Making exceptions undermines the integrity of the corporate requirements for stage-gate approval. The proverb of the camel's nose in the tent really applies here. Let the camel put its nose in the tent and soon the entire camel will be in the tent and you will be on the outside.

The corporate requirements for stage-gates are there to increase the chances of maximizing business value, to eliminate bias from portfolio selection, or to protect the shareholders from loss. If a requirement does none of those things, it should be eliminated so that teams are not overburdened with work. If an investment committee is constantly being asked for exceptions for noncompliance, there may be a problem that is fixable. Are project sponsors or project managers even aware of the requirement? Does the team have the resources to get the job done? In this example of the MOU, is the commercial group getting involved early enough? If a requirement, while desirable, is not feasible to achieve consistently, the requirement should be eliminated, and the corporation will have to live with the risk.

Companies best at doing capital projects have regular corporate reviews of the stage-gate requirements to ensure that they are not excessive. Stage-gate requirements tend to build up over time, so a regular review is a useful exercise.

# 12 Executive Role, Executive Control: 12 Essential Rules

You, an executive responsible for a capital project, may be in a tough position. Your decisions and actions have an enormous influence on the value delivered by the capital project; yet, you may not have much understanding of how capital projects are developed and executed, what your role is in the whole activity, and how you should perform it.

In this book, I have laid out the essential concepts you need to know and given some practical advice on what you need to do. In this chapter, I summarize the rules you can use to avoid costly mistakes and make your projects pay off.

## Rule 1: Use the Stage-Gate Process

Ask yourself a few questions: *Do I want the best chance at identifying and delivering the maximum value from a capital project? Do I want to make good decisions that prudently balance risk and reward, cost and benefit?* Of course you do. Projects that adhere to the principles of a well-designed stage-gate process, on average, deliver the value expected at authorization. Projects that do not, on average, lose about half the promised value.

Executives provide the leadership, discipline, timely input, resources, and time needed to complete the work that is part of the process.

## Rule 2: Start by Framing the Project

The project frame forces a disciplined approach to defining the opportunity or problem to be solved and a comprehensive look at all the things a business wants to accomplish with a project. It is the foundation for all the work that follows. The project frame identifies what the opportunity is—and what it is not. The project frame guards against the tendency to move too quickly to identify the solution. Locking into options too quickly can cut off alternatives that would generate more value or it can start a project down a path that is not going to work. A project frame also brings organizational alignment around the project, its objectives, and its strategies.

The most critical time for executive involvement is when the project frame is developed. This is the point in time when executives make the strategic decisions that will shape and direct the project going forward.

## Rule 3: Ensure Project Sponsor Involvement

The project sponsor is the single point of accountability for the value identified and delivered by a project. Effective use of the stage-gate process is very difficult without a project sponsor. The project sponsor is the force that drives for a robust business case, clears barriers and fixes problems outside the control of the project manager, and ensures that everything is in place to start making money when the asset is ready to be handed over to users or operations.

The project sponsor is an executive role on major investments. More senior executives also have an important job to do. They choose the project sponsor, establish the project sponsor's mandate, and hold project sponsors accountable for their performance.

## Rule 4: Develop Clear Objectives

Objectives describe what the business wants to accomplish with a project. The objectives establish the criteria used to make all project decisions, and they measure whether a project was successful. Clear objectives are comprehensive, quantified, and prioritized. Clear objectives provide a coherent set of instructions to the project team on how to develop the project. Considerable work is required to develop clear objectives. Objectives start out as aspiration statements that are progressively refined into the quantitative targets used to measure performance. There will be some back and forth as the economic and technical analysis done on the project identifies what is possible, where trade-offs need to be made, and what is simply not realistic.

Executives have to stay engaged as the project frame is developed and, later, as the project is developed, giving input and making timely decisions.

## Rule 5: Invest in Owner Teams and Provide the Support They Need

An owner project team, adequately resourced and functionally integrated, is an investment that pays off in better, faster, and cheaper projects. Robust owner teams complete the work specified in the stage-gate process more effectively, they are able to develop and execute strategies to maximize value, and they can spot and manage emerging risks better than less capable teams.

The project manager has the lead role in identifying the team structure, the skills and competencies required, and the people they want on the team. Executives work with the project manager to understand the requirements, and, ultimately, provide the resources, finances, and oftentimes people from their own organization to staff the team. Executives work closely with the project manager to develop staffing strategies when there are shortages of key personnel.

The project manager also has the lead role in building the team into a cohesive unit that is aligned around a shared set of objectives. Executives, however, have an important role in bringing the team together. Executives supply the vision for the project and explain

why the project is important to the business. Project teams need
to understand both to make the personal commitment to the
project.

Executives regularly interact with the project team and challenge
the project team to find ways to increase the value created by the
project. They also coach and mentor team members through rough
periods and are ready to step in to assist when needed.

## Rule 6: Reach a Strong Level of Project Definition

The quality of project definition at authorization is the best indicator
of whether a project will come in on time and on budget and deliver an
asset that meets specifications. Projects with strong definition, on
average, do not lose value from cost and schedule overruns or asset
technical performance shortfalls. In contrast, projects with weak
project definition, on average, erode 25 percent of the value expected
at authorization and are much more vulnerable to being disaster
projects with bad cost, schedule, *and* asset performance. A project
with strong definition has a one in ten chance of eroding more than
50 percent of the expected value (a disaster). The odds increase to one
in four with weak definition. Executives ultimately determine what
level of project definition a project achieves. They approve project
strategies that will or will not allow a project team to complete the
work needed to achieve strong definition. In addition, executives who
control stage-gates decide whether a project with weak definition can
move to the next project stage.

Executives should understand that the decision to allow a project
to be authorized with weak definition is a strategic decision. The trade-
off being made is that the value gained by forgoing strong project
definition (higher revenue, operating profit) to save time, money, or
both exceeds the inefficiency and the risk associated with weak
definition. This decision has to be carefully weighed because,

historically, the costs and project risks from weak definition are often underestimated.

## Rule 7: Factor the Accuracy of the Capital Cost Estimate into Decision Making

Capital cost estimates are usually more uncertain than executives realize. This is especially true with early capital cost estimates, which tend to be too low. Until the project scope is fully understood, cost estimators will have a difficult time developing a reliable base estimate range for any cost estimate.

Executives have to engage with the project manager and cost estimator to understand the range of the estimate, what is included in the estimate and what is not, and the major assumptions used to develop the estimate. To make informed project decisions, executives need to have a realistic understanding not only of the chances of an overrun but also of the potential magnitude of an overrun.

## Rule 8: Set Contingency in Accordance with Project Risk

Contingency should be set at a level that produces an equal chance of an overrun or underrun of the budget given to the project team to complete a project. Adding too much contingency to a cost estimate reduces the discipline needed to challenge and scrutinize expenditures. Adding too little contingency either forces money up into the base estimate where it cannot be controlled or exposes the project to a greater chance of an overrun.

Executives have to engage with the project team to understand the basis of the contingency estimate and to decide what is needed for that particular project.

## Rule 9: Build an Effective Steering Committee

A steering committee brings together the subject-matter expertise a project sponsor needs to make good strategic project decisions. The steering committee membership should be limited to the leaders of the organizations that are key stakeholders in the project. The committee should be as small as possible to make decision making easier but with enough representation to get adequate input on important issues. The project sponsor should have the final decision-making authority so their accountability for the project is not diluted.

To be effective, a steering committee, like any other team, requires clear roles and responsibilities as well as commitment from the team members to prepare for and to participate in meetings. Each meeting should have a formal agenda, decisions should be documented, and responsibility for action items should be assigned and followed up on.

## Rule 10: Use a Robust Risk Management Process

A robust a risk management process provides executives with insight into major project risks. Using the process in a collaborative, transparent way provides a mechanism for executives to align with the project team on the chances a risk event will occur and the possible consequences if it does. Executives can then decide how the risks should be managed.

However, executives have to recognize that risk management is not a substitute for strong project definition. Risks that are not known, sometimes referred to as *unknown unknowns,* cannot be managed. Project definition activities change *unknown unknowns* into *known unknowns,* which are risks you can manage.

## Rule 11: Keep the Stage-Gates Strong

A stage-gate process with weak gates will not work. The primary document executives examine to make stage-gate decisions is the project's business case. The business case explains the justification for the project and summarizes the investment analysis used to evaluate the project's potential profitability and risk. Without strong stage-gates, the business cases presented to executives will tend to overstate benefits and understate risk. Only strong stage-gates will ensure that the rigor and discipline needed to produce reliable estimates happens consistently.

Senior executives, starting with the CEO, establish the requirements for the completeness and quality of work that must be completed at each stage-gate. They decide what information is needed to make a good investment decision at each stage-gate. They then have to create an accountability mechanism to ensure the requirements are met.

## Rule 12: Be Coachable

One last piece of advice. Capital projects are complicated. Very few people have all the knowledge and skills needed to complete every step in the process. You have to be open and acknowledge when there is something you do not understand. Have the project manager or project team explain why some activity in project definition is important, why they need a decision right now, or what the risks of making a change to objectives later in the project are. You are not giving up control or authority by asking questions or encouraging healthy debate. Fostering an environment of mutual respect and trust will only improve a project. Let the project team and other executives supporting the project coach you on your role. Do this and you will be more effective, you will sleep better at night, and you might even have some fun!

# GLOSSARY

**asset** Property, plant, and equipment used to generate profit.

**asset performance shortfall** Inability of the asset created or modified by the project to perform according to specifications. The dimensions of asset performance include rates of production, product or service quality, and level of operating costs.

**Assess stage** The first stage of the stage-gate process. The primary activities in the Assess stage are to complete the project frame, identify options for achieving the business case, and develop the initial business case.

**authorization decision** The decision to proceed into the Execute stage. Although the authorization decision is not irreversible, stopping a project after it starts Execute will result in considerable sunk costs that rapidly escalate to 50 percent of the total budget or higher.

**authorization** The release of the full capital budget to the project team to complete the project. Authorization typically occurs at Gate 3 in the stage-gate process.

**base case** The results of the investment analysis used to evaluate profitability and risk of a project using the most likely option or alternative.

**boundary conditions** Specify the limits to the opportunity and the potential dimensions of the capital project to achieve business objectives.

**business case** Explains the business justification for the project, documents the objectives and key performance targets, describes the project scope and strategy, and summarizes the investment analysis.

**business objectives** Describe the fundamental reason a business wants to do a project.

**capital cost** The total cost of a project needed to create or to modify an asset to bring it to commercially operable status.

**capital project** Investments of substantial company resources to develop, to improve, or to refurbish an asset that is expected to generate cash flows for more than one year.

**contingency**   Money added to a cost estimate to reduce risk of an overrun of the cost estimate.

**current condition**   The current capacity or capability of a business to produce a product or service.

**decision criteria**   Specify how executives will chose between options and decide whether to approve the project for the next stage in the stage-gate process.

**Define stage**   The third stage of the stage-gate process. The primary activities in the Define stage are the completion of the preliminary asset technical design and project execution plans.

**estimate accuracy**   An indication of the degree by which the final cost outcome may deviate from the single point value used as the estimated cost for the project.

**execution**   The period from the time the project definition is complete until the asset is installed and put into service. The primary activities in execution include completing the asset technical design, ordering and receiving project goods and services, and building/assembling the asset created or modified by the project.

**Front-End Loading (FEL)**   The first three stages of the stage-gate process.

**functionally integrated team**   All the skills needed to complete a project are present on the project team at the right time and each of the team members has the ability and authority to perform their role.

**givens**   Absolutes that any aspect of the project cannot violate.

**governance structure**   The rules and delegation of authority for making project decisions.

**investment analysis**   The evaluation of a project for profitability and risk.

**investment committee**   Makes the stage-gate decision to allow a project to pass to the next stage.

**management reserve**   Management reserve is money added to the capital cost estimate used in the project's investment analysis (but discretely funded) but is not released to the project team until needed. Management reserve is for identified risks that may or may not materialize.

**market analysis**   The analysis to define an opportunity. The market analysis includes price and demand forecasts, assessment of potential competitor actions, and identification of customer or consumer requirements.

**net present value (NPV)**   The present value of future cash flows discounted at the appropriate cost of capital, minus the initial net cash outlay.

**performance gap**   The difference between the current condition and the target condition.

**portfolio**   A set of capital projects developed and executed by a company or a business unit within a company.

**project controls**   Include the activities that track actual project performance against the plan by collecting data, comparing to the plan, documenting the variance, and using the data to recommend corrective actions and to develop forecasts of the likely outcomes.

**project definition**   The process of converting business objectives into a project scope and strategy to design, build, and install the asset created or modified by the project to achieve the objectives.

**project frame**   A project frame is a clear explanation of the opportunity or problem being solved, what the business hopes to accomplish with the opportunity, and the plan for moving forward.

**project life cycle**   The period between the start of the Assess stage to the handover of the asset to the user or the operations group.

**project objectives**   The means for achieving business objectives.

**project scope of work**   All work required to deliver an asset with the specified features and functions.

**project sponsor**   The chief proponent of the project from the organization requesting the capital for the project.

**return on investment**   The profit or loss resulting from a capital project, usually expressed as an annual percentage return.

**risk**   An uncertain event that, if it occurs, has a positive or negative effect on one or more objectives.

**risk management**   The process of identifying individual risks, understanding and analyzing them, and then managing them.

**Select stage**   The second stage of the stage-gate process. The primary activity of the Select stage is to develop the full scope of work required to achieve the business objectives.

**stage-gates**   Discrete stopping points built into the project delivery process that give executives the opportunity to review the merits of a capital project to decide whether money should be invested in pursuing an opportunity.

**stakeholder**   Any person or organization who is affected by the opportunity and who can affect the shape of the opportunity itself.

**steering committee**   An advisory committee to support project sponsor decision making.

**sunk costs**   A cost that has already been incurred and cannot be recovered.

**target condition**   The desired capacity or capability of a business to produce a product or service after the project is complete.

**value**   The profits or benefits created by a capital project after accounting for the total cost of the project.

**value erosion or value loss**   The difference between the expected value when the project was funded and what was actually delivered.

**Value Improving Practices (VIPs)**   Out-of-the-ordinary practices used to improve cost, schedule, and/or asset performance of capital projects.

**variable production costs**   Expenses that vary in direct proportion to the level of production.

# INDEX

Printed and bound by CPI Group (UK) Ltd, Croydon, CR0 4YY

16/04/2025

14658519-0001